In the future
everyone will be dead
for 15 minutes.

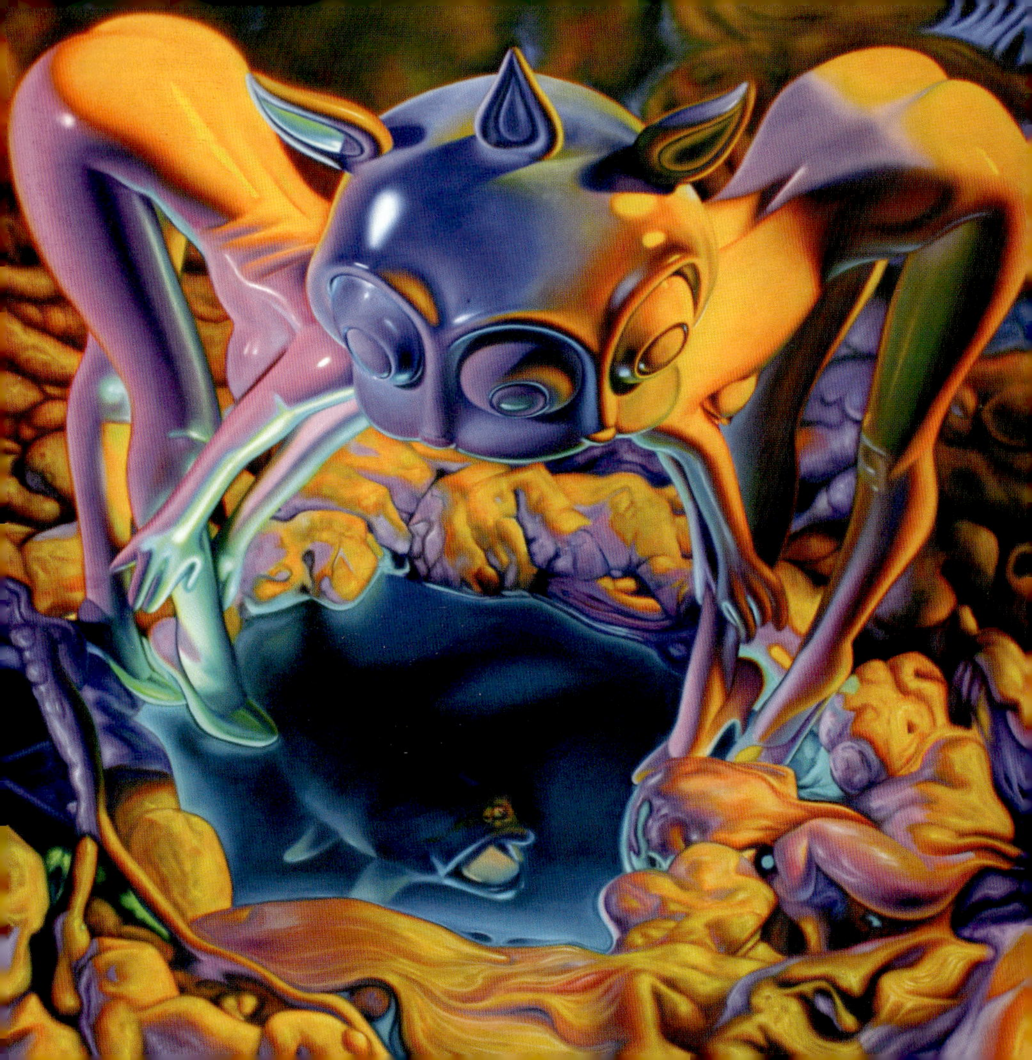

FAUXLOSOPHY

Quotable quotes. The building blocks of wisdom. Bite size nuggets of insight that pave the road to understanding. The life blood of philosophy. The nails that hold together universal truth. And occasionally erroneous bull shit.

Lightning never strikes twice. Unless you're the Empire State building, which is struck an average of 25 times a year. The definition of a fool is someone who does the same thing over and over again expecting different results. In my experience I have been arrested for certain behavior on one day and greatly rewarded for the same behavior on another. I have repeated my actions and assumptions (though the circumstances changed) and gotten different results. Therefore I am the definition of a fool, a fact I will not argue with because anyone who argues with a fool may be mistaken for one.

Belief is truth, truth is the most believable lie, and fauxlosophy is the most memorable pronouncements of the true believer.

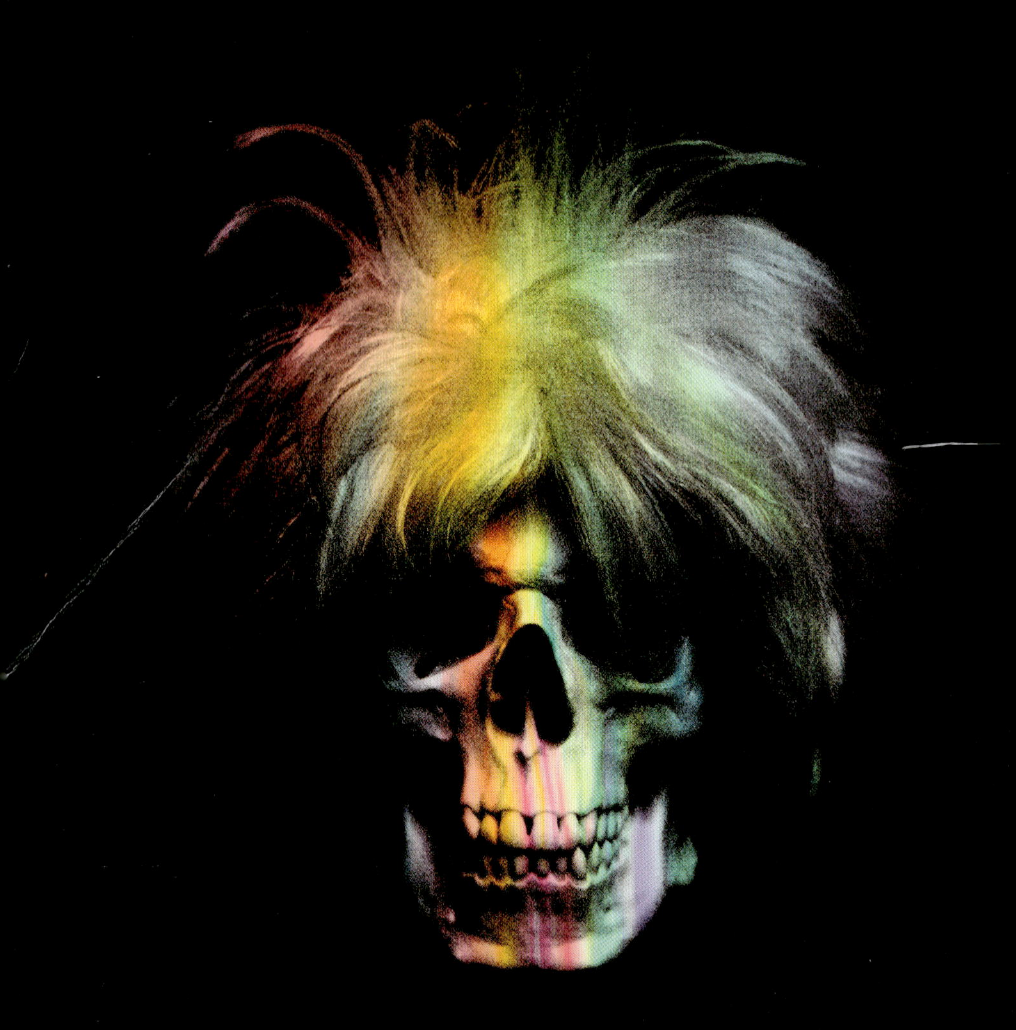

A catalogue record for this book is available from the British Library.

First Edition 2016

First published in Great Britain in 2016 by Carpet Bombing Culture.

An imprint of Pro-actif Communications

www.carpetbombingculture.co.uk

email: books@carpetbombingculture.co.uk

ISBN - 978-1-908211-45-3

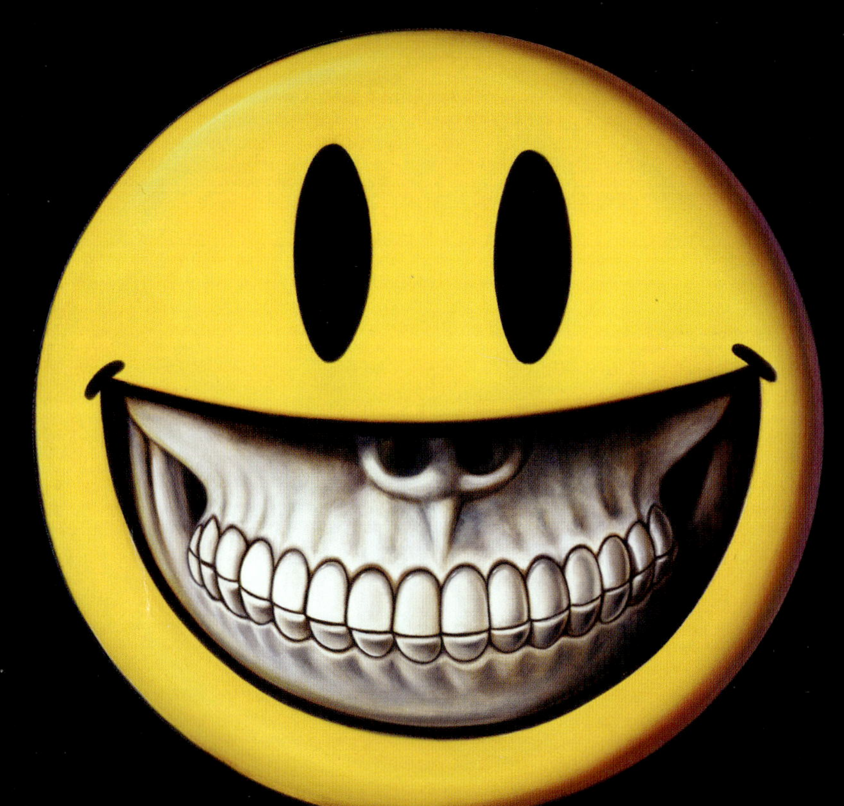

My reflections always get it backwards.

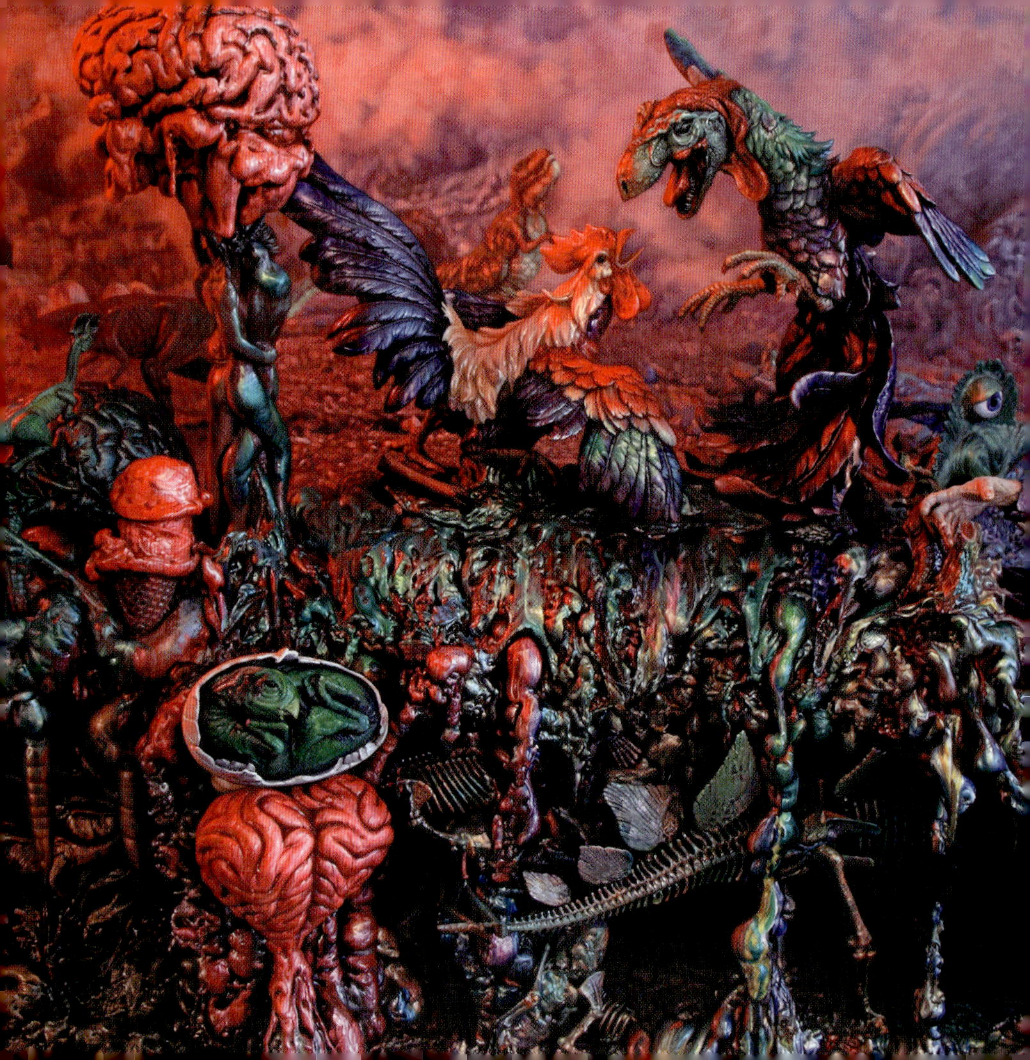

Evolution is the myth that keeps on morphing.

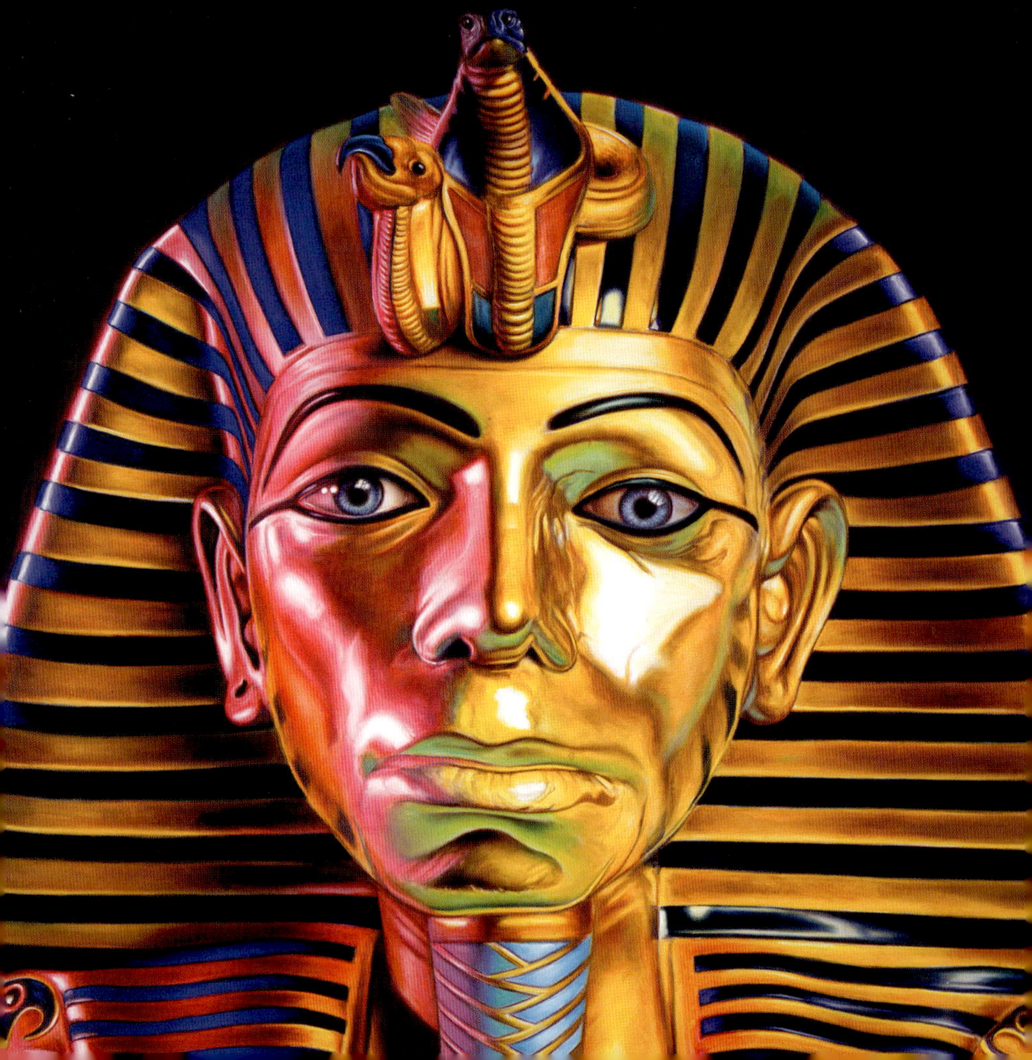

Narcissism makes me feel better about myself.

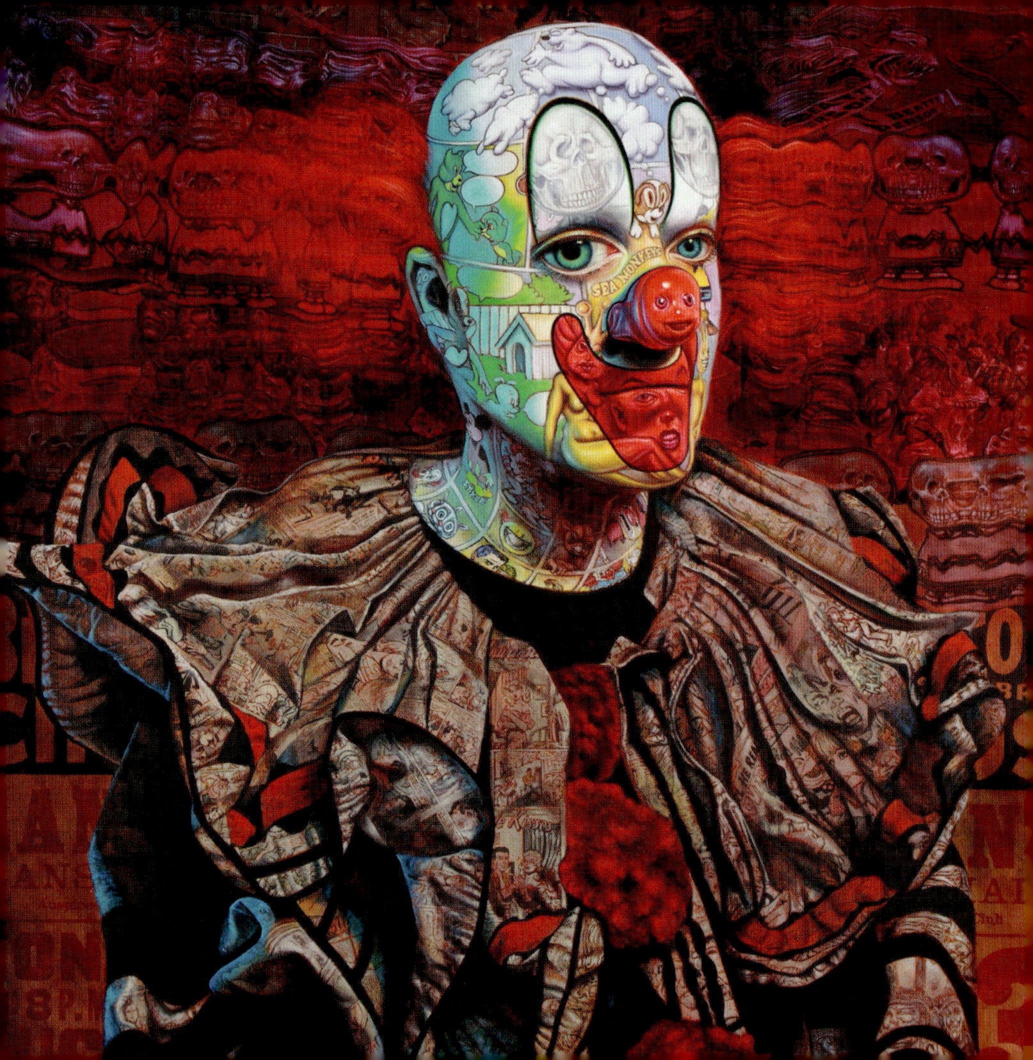
SEA MONKEYS

Fame always finds the village idiot.

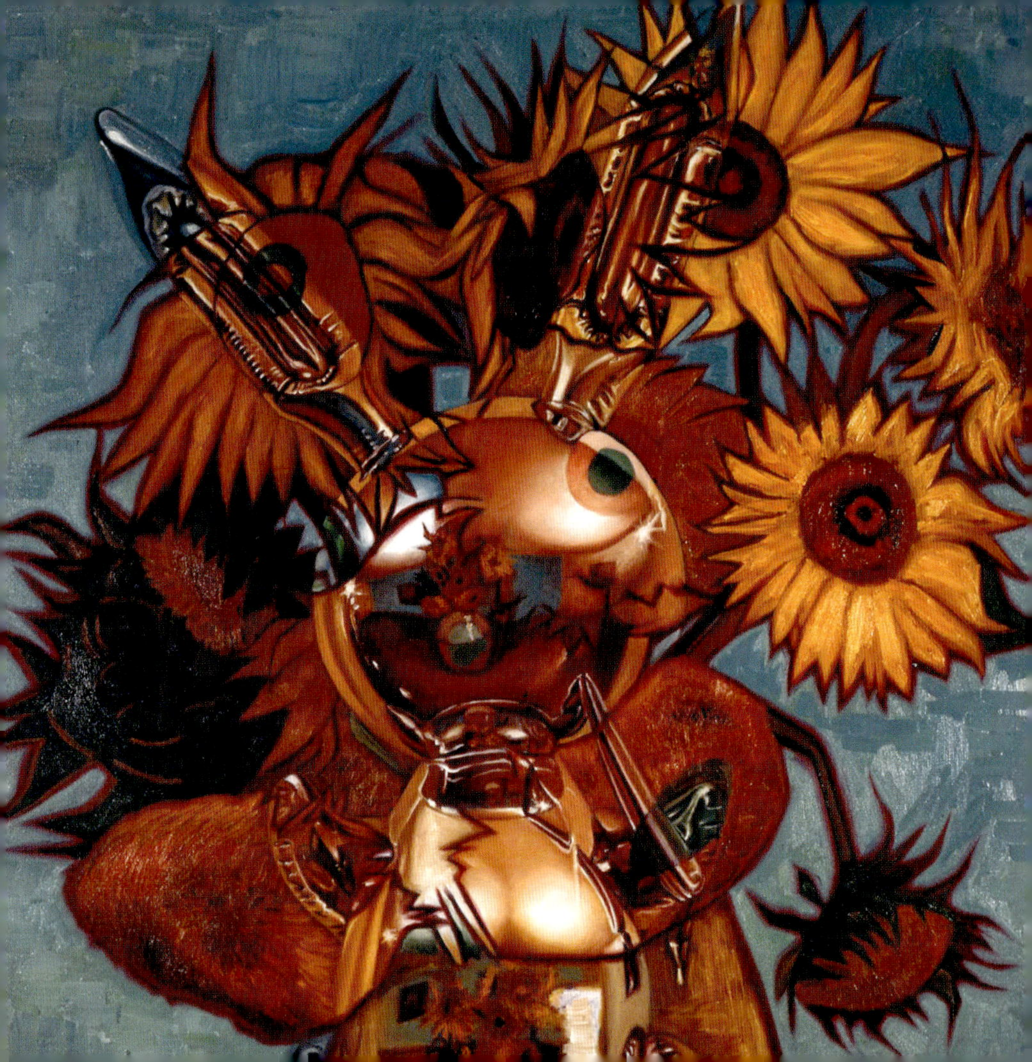

Art is the canary in the goldmine.

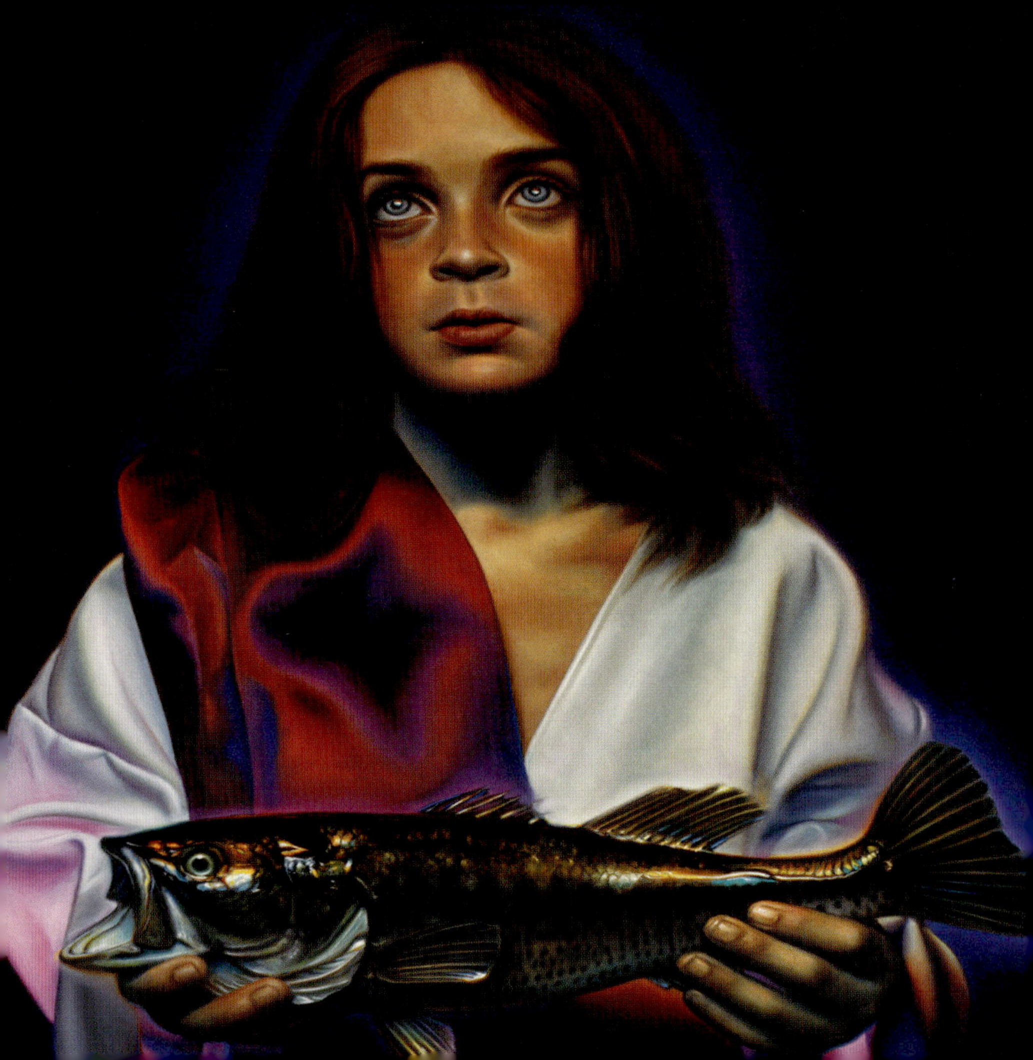

Sell a man a fish and he will eat for a day.

Teach a man to fish and he will put you out of a job.

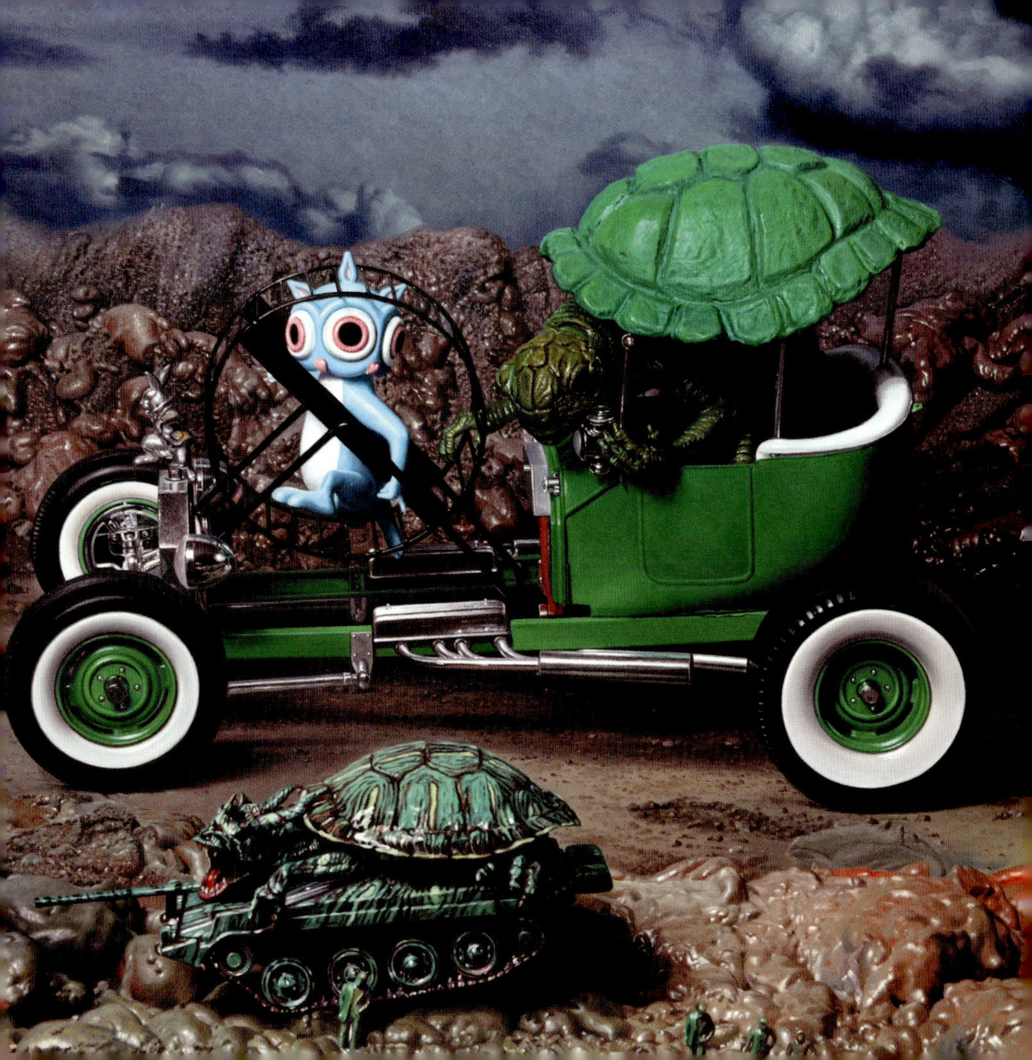

Last place is first place in the very next race.

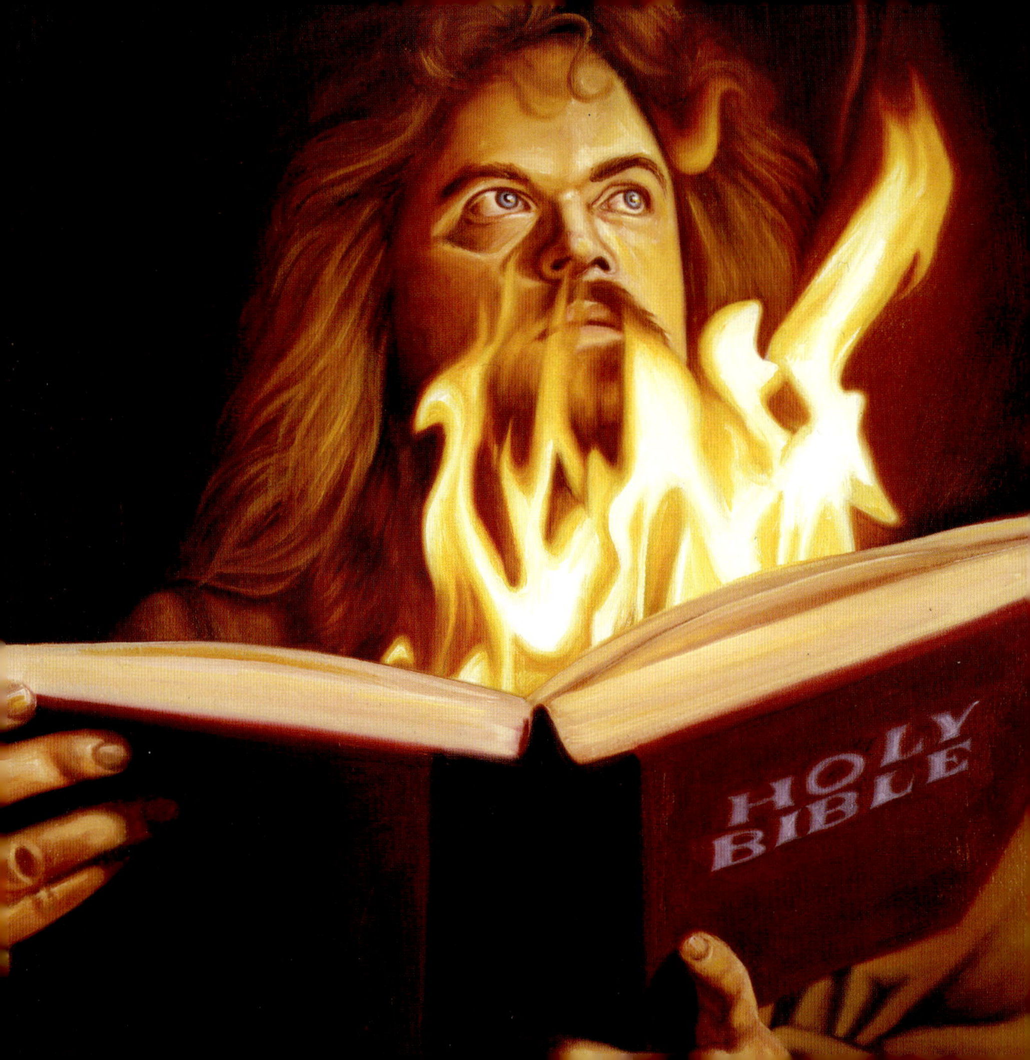
HOLY
BIBLE

You can’t judge a book while it’s on fire.

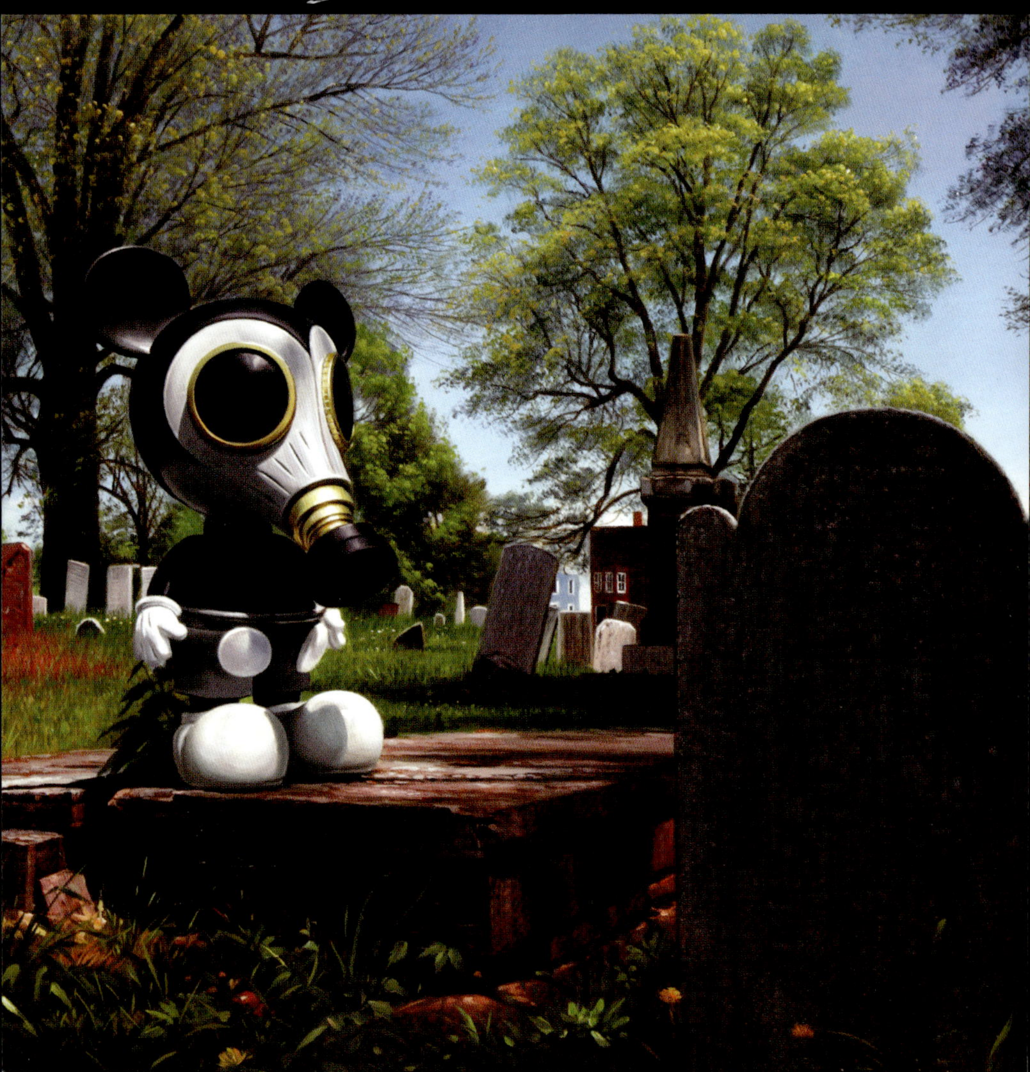

You don’t protest air pollution by holding your breath.

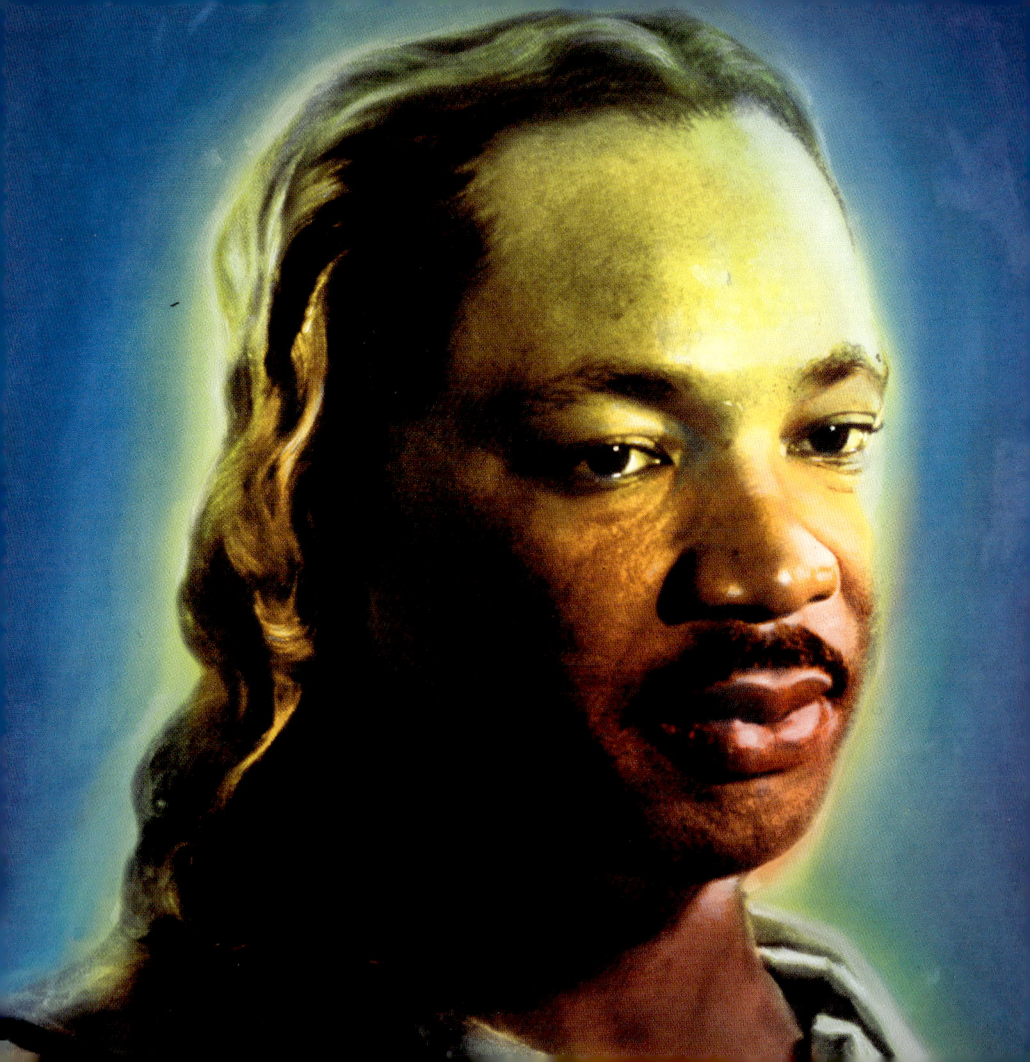

There's nothing to dream about in Heaven.

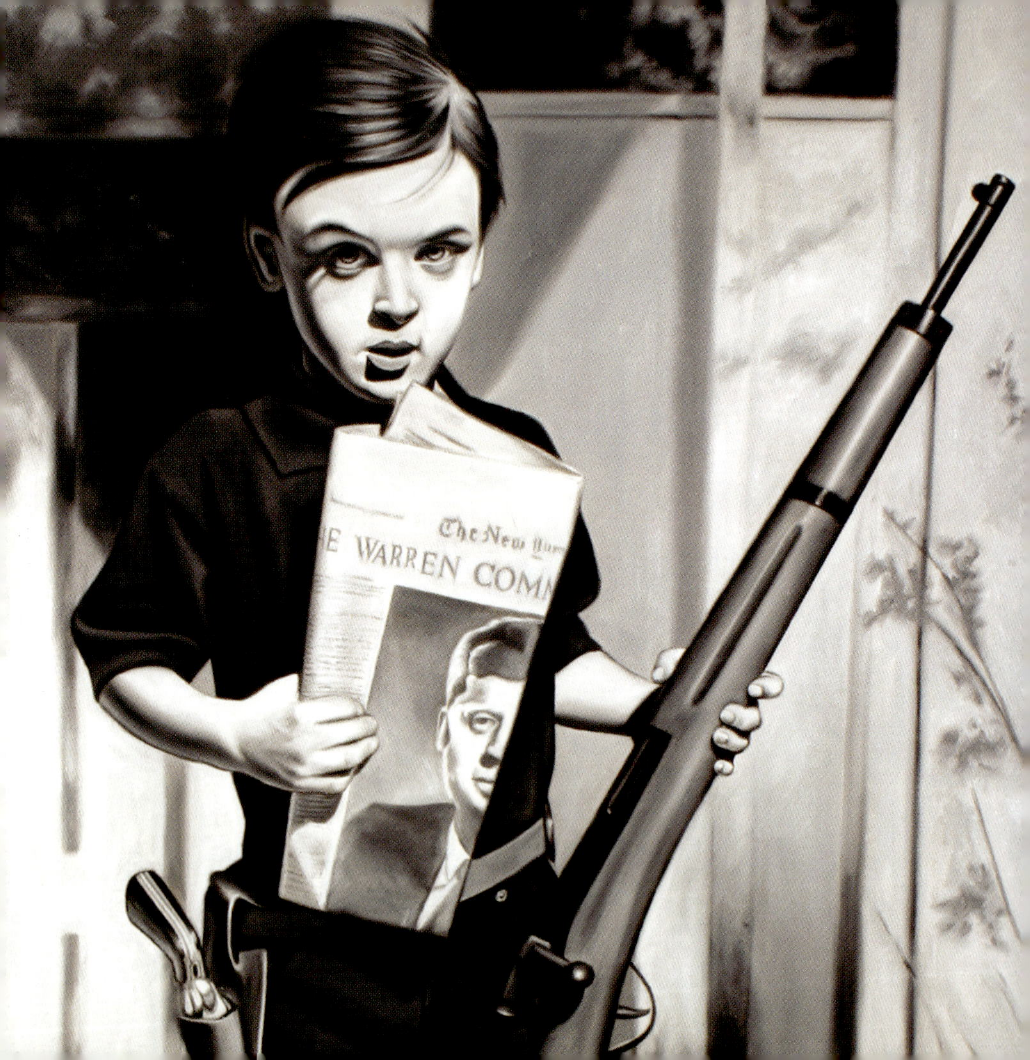

The New York
HE WARREN COMM

Criminals are
the product of
arrested development.

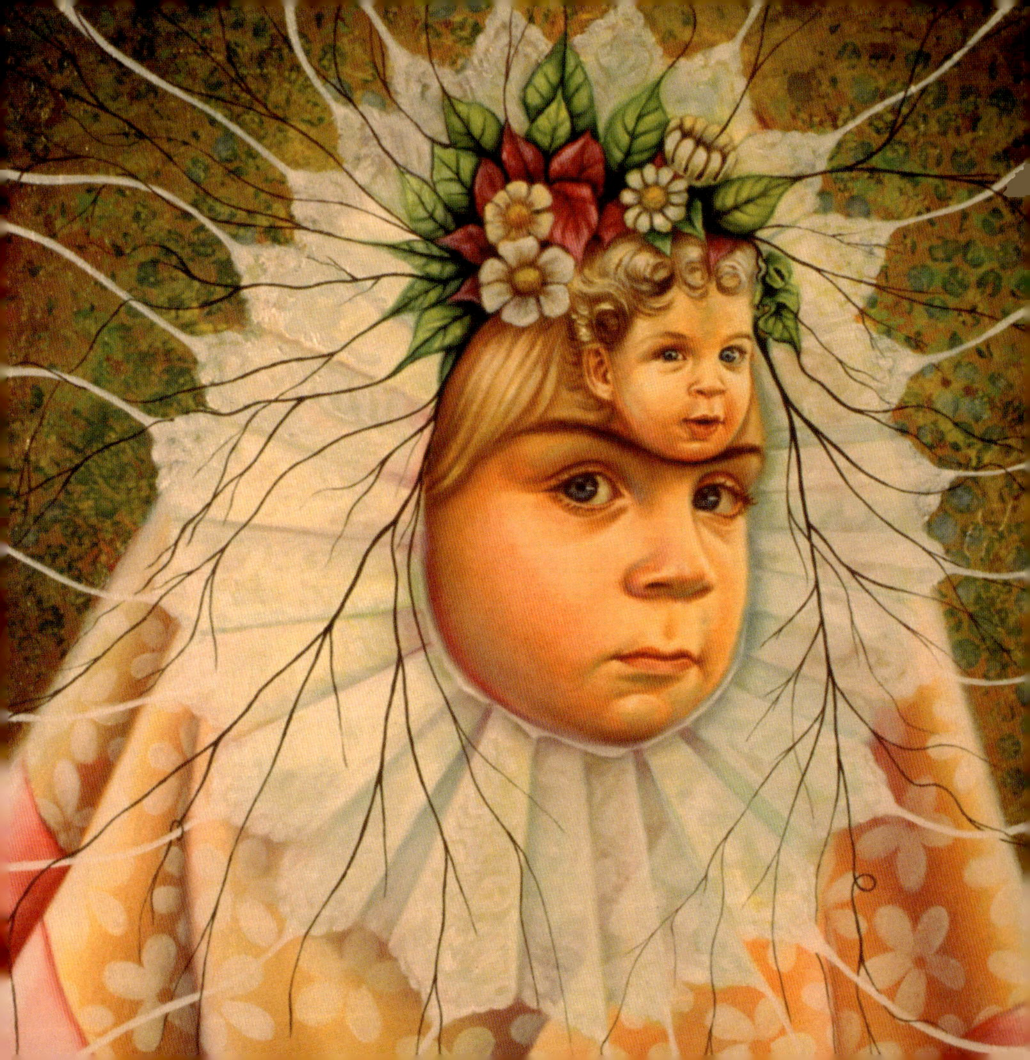

Familiarity is the enemy of admiration.

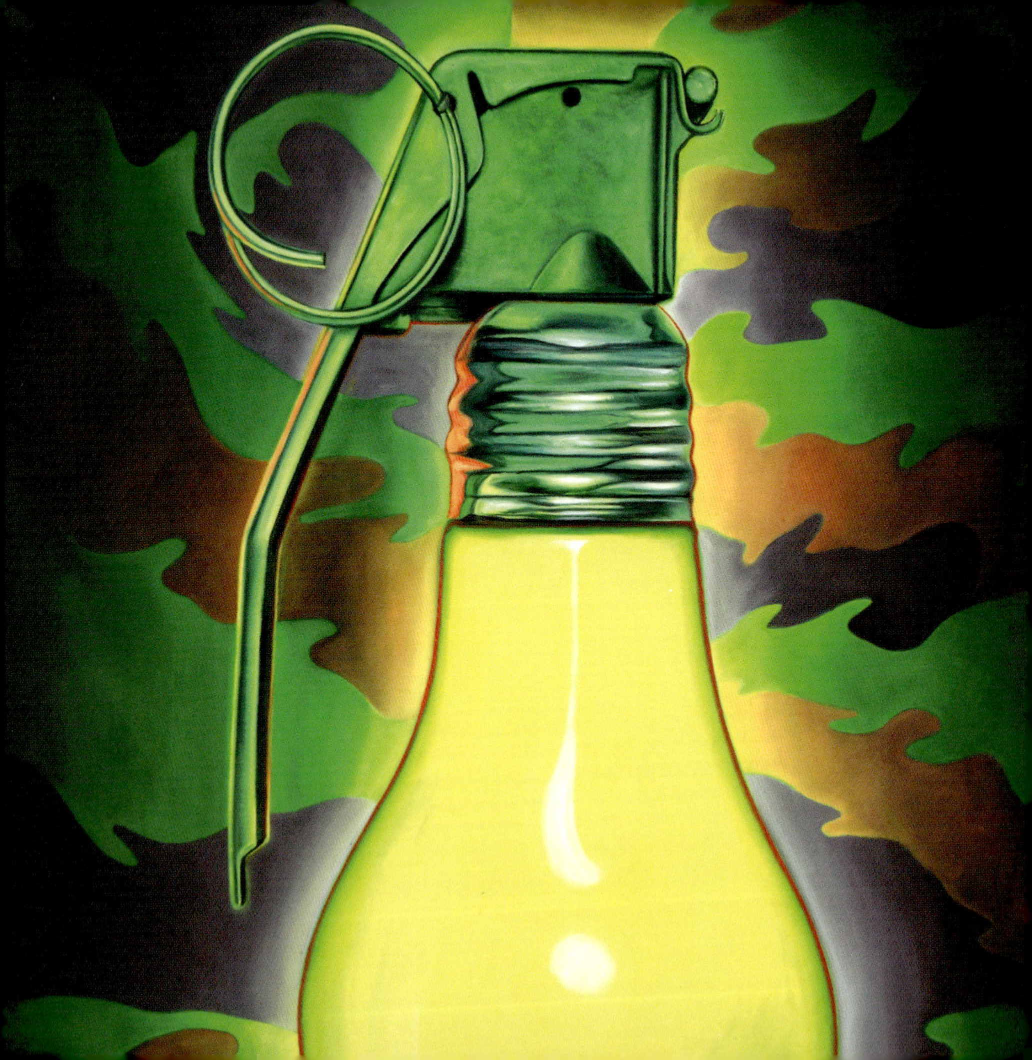

There's nothing more dangerous than a good idea.

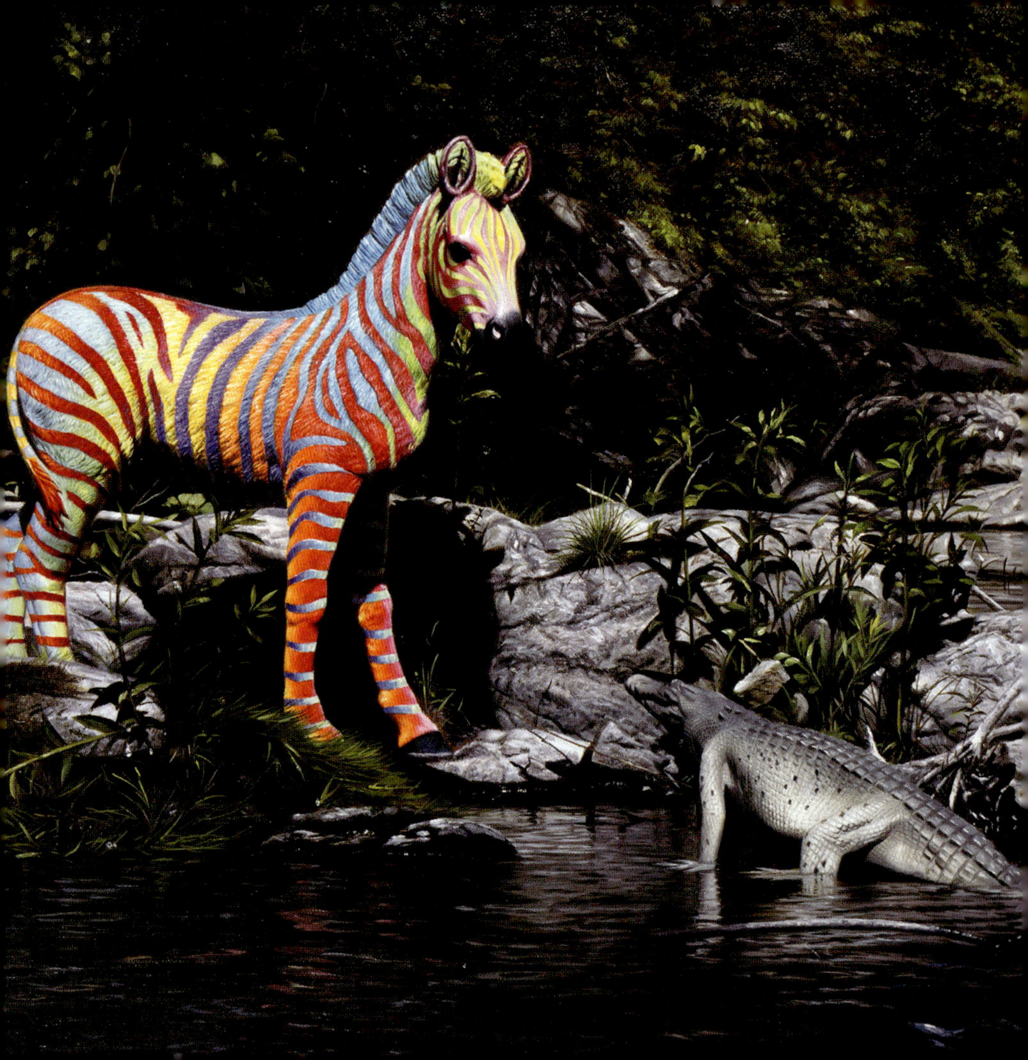

You can lead a horse to Harvard but you can't make him think.

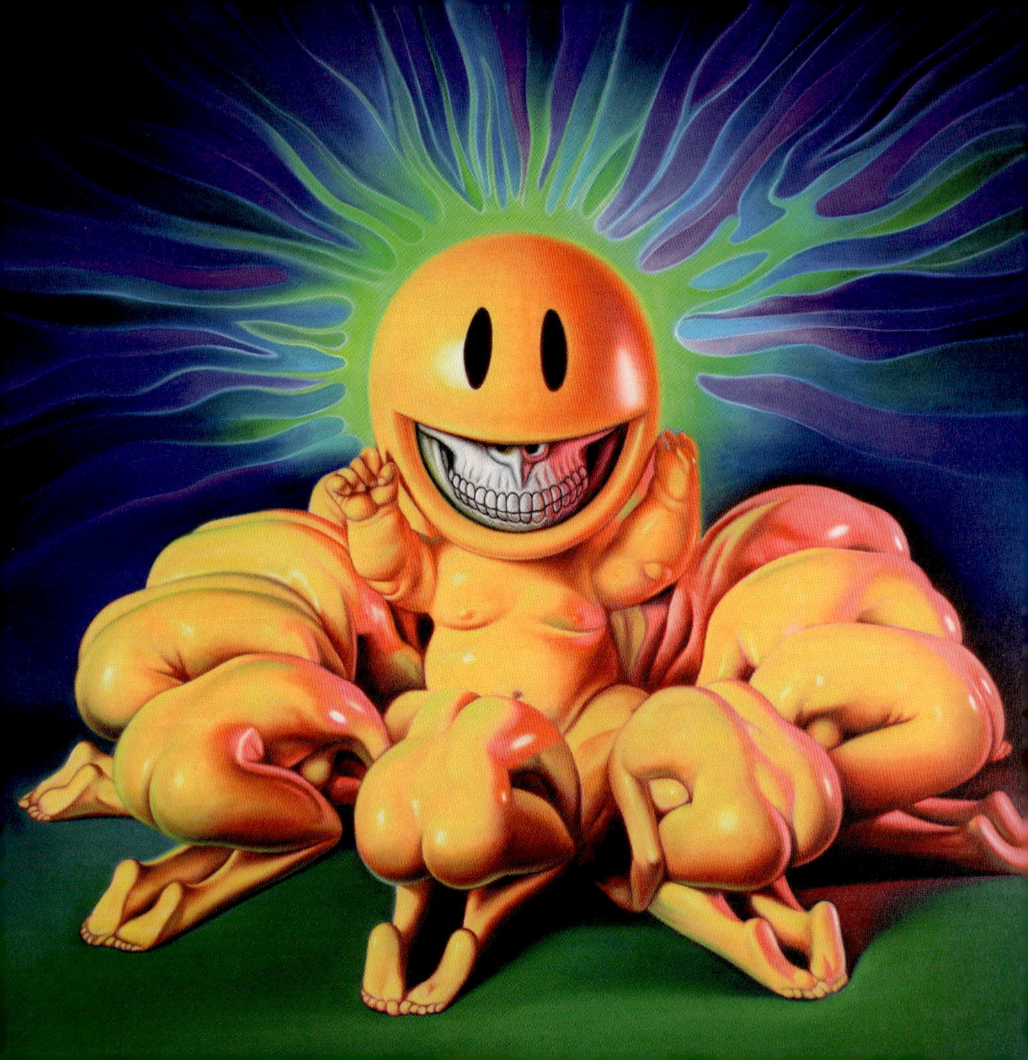

The only ass I follow is my own.

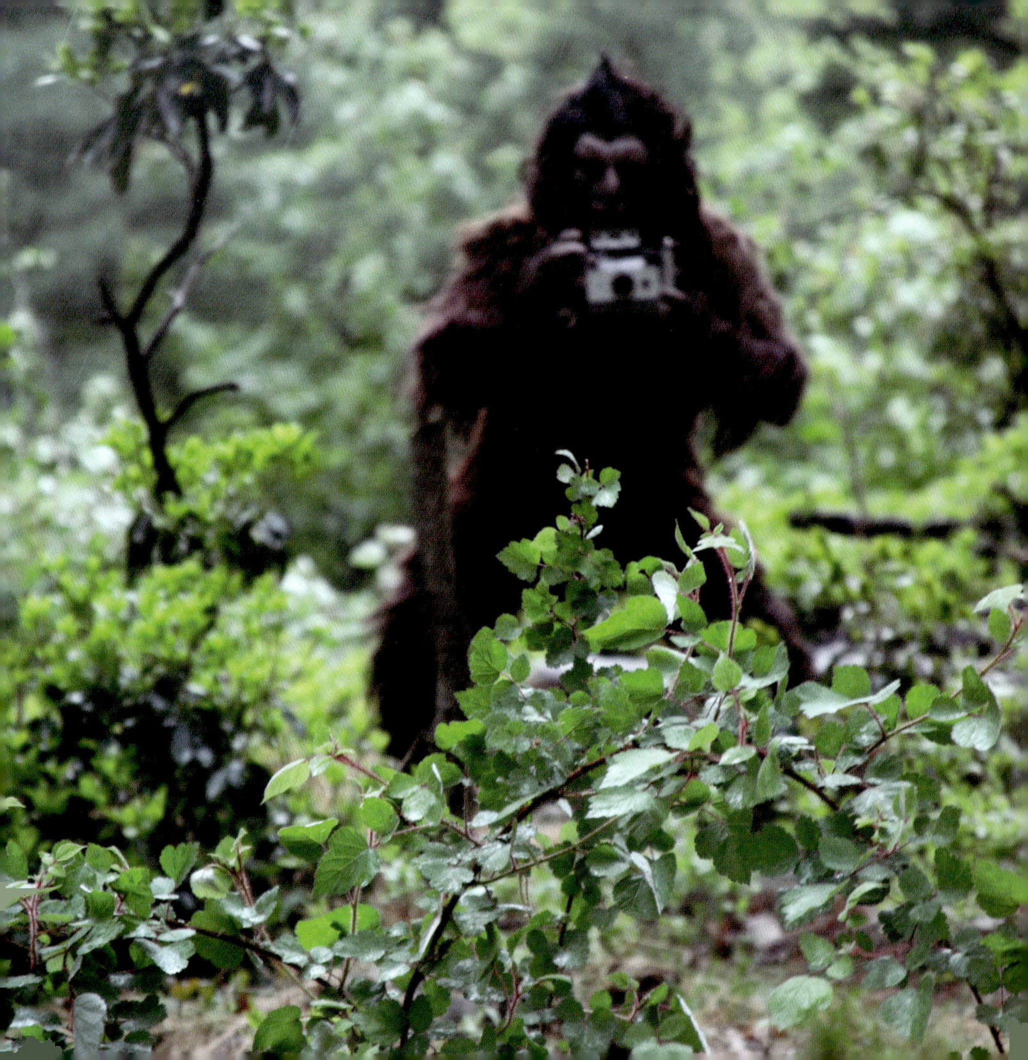

**If you believe,
it doesn't have to
be true.**

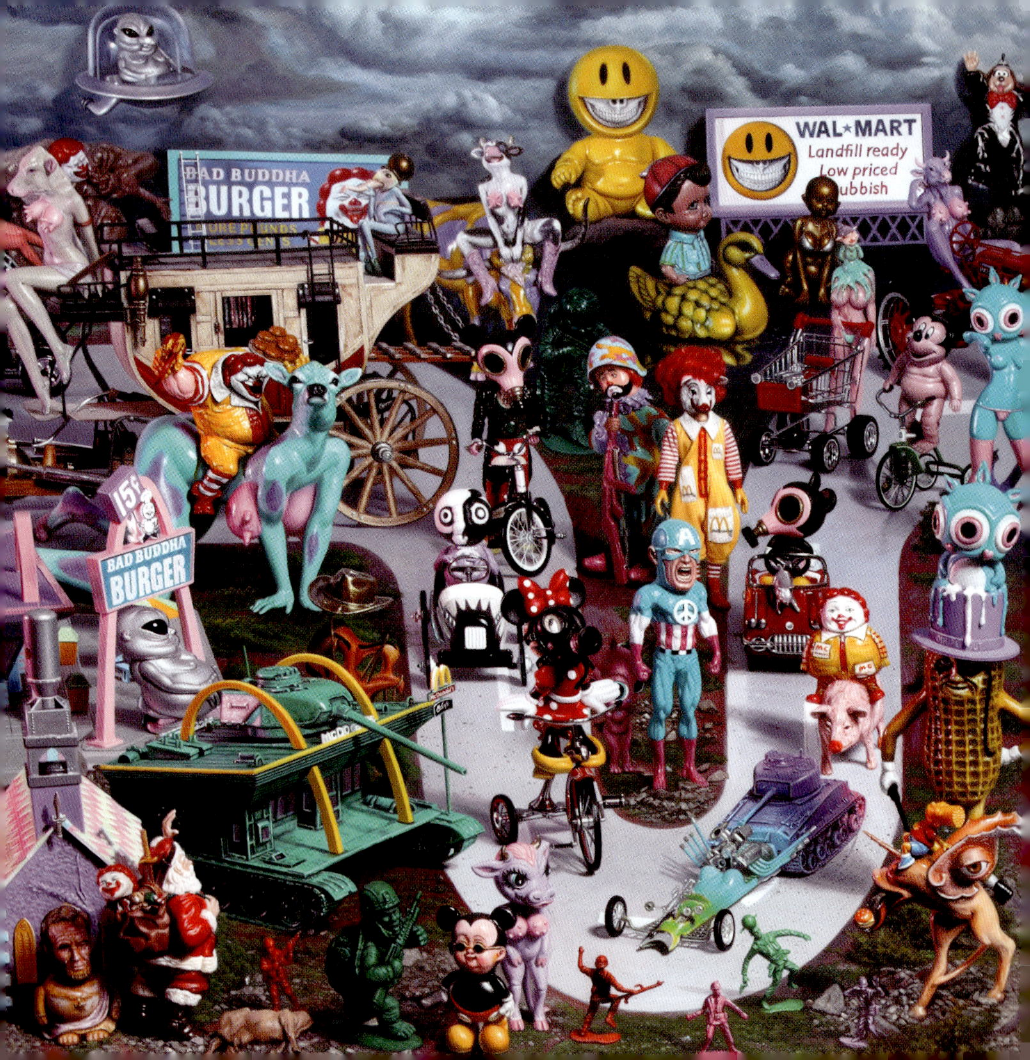
BAD BUDDHA
BURGER
WAL★MART
Landfill ready
Low priced
15¢
BAD BUDDHA
BURGER

Footprints go unnoticed on a well worn path.

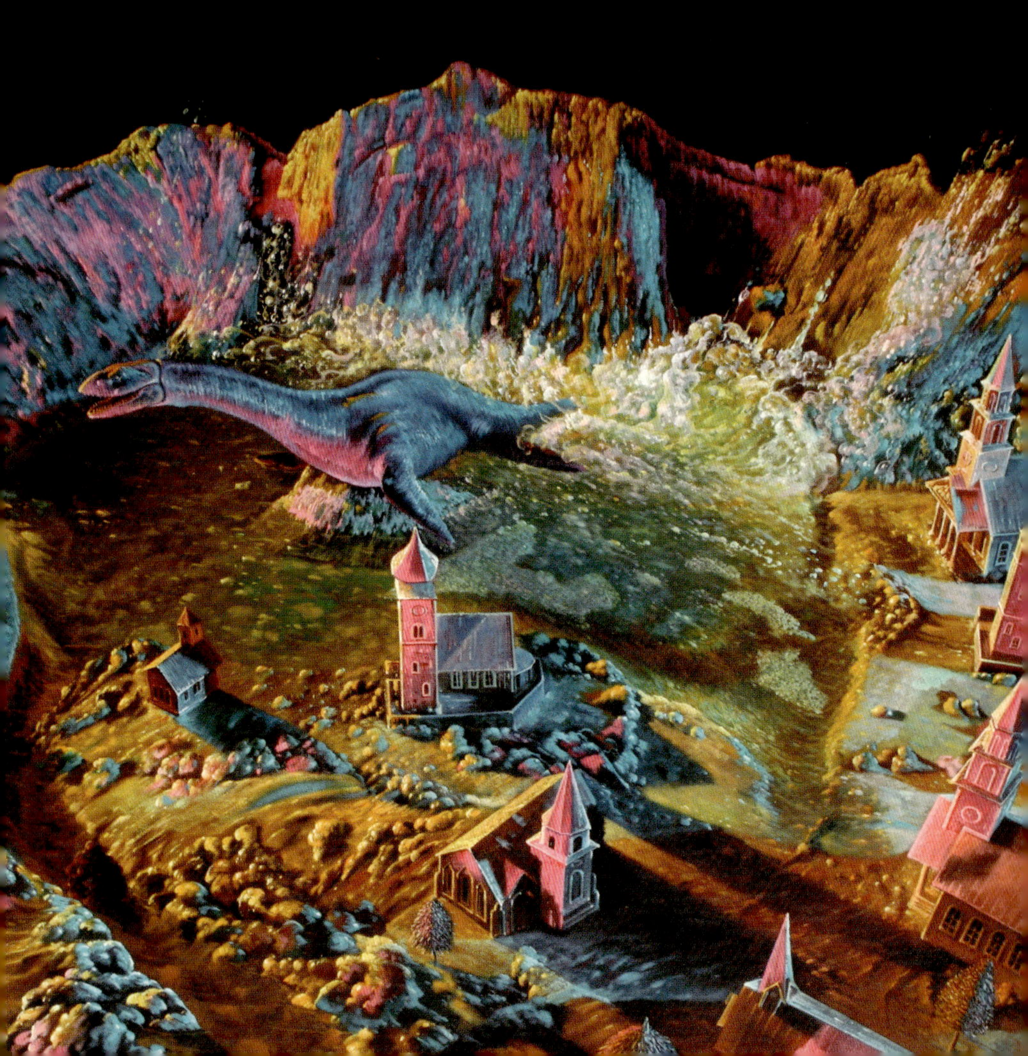

You can't part the waters without making some waves.

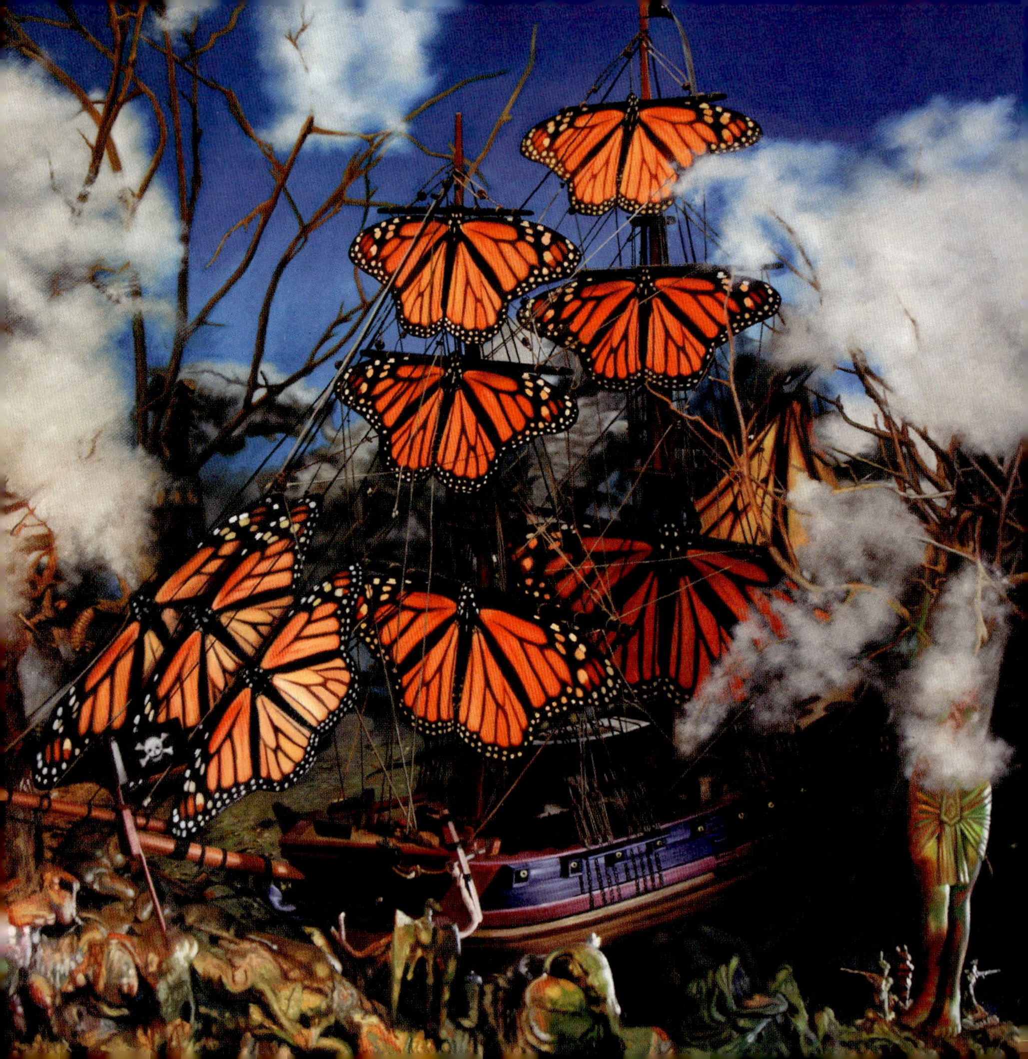

The end of the world goes on forever.

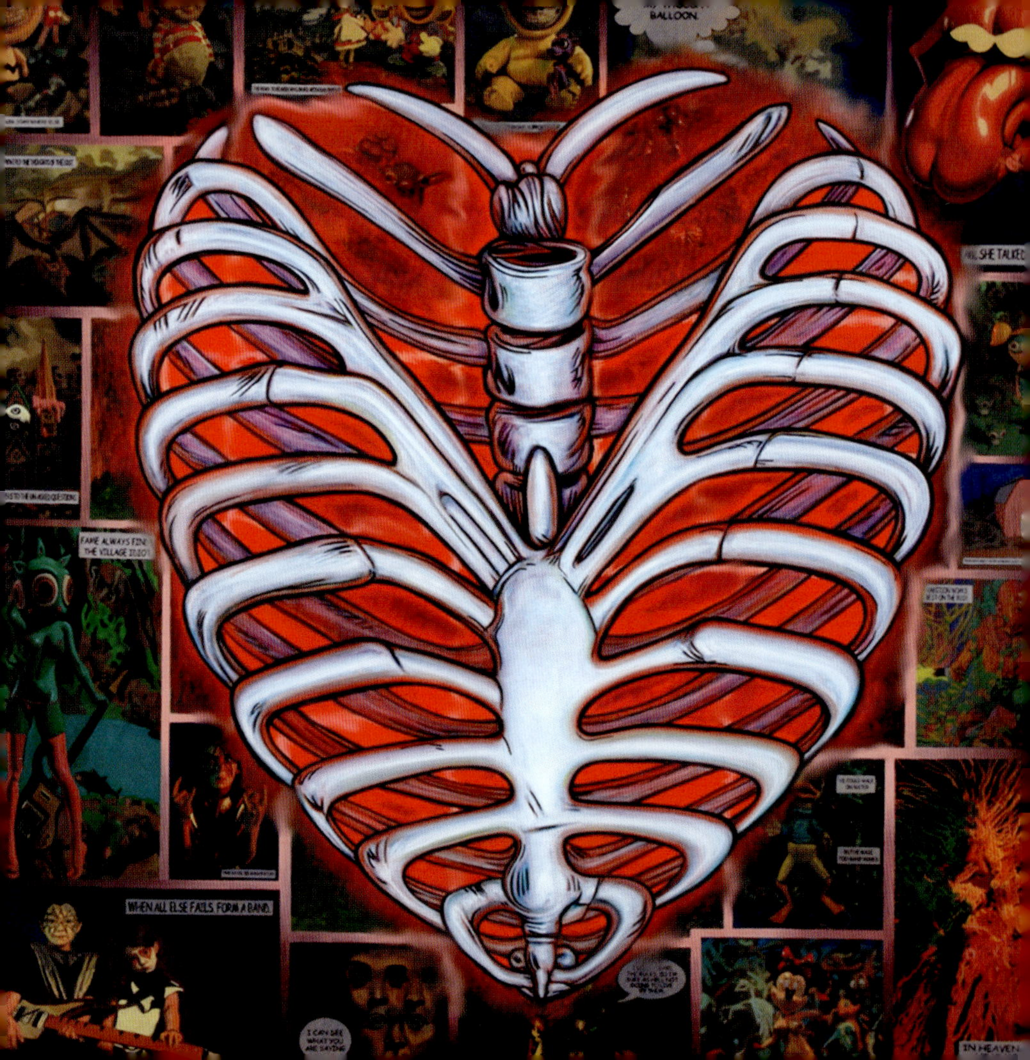
BALLOON.
WHEN ALL ELSE FAILS, FORM A BAND.
IN HEAVEN

My heart is in the right place...

between my lungs.

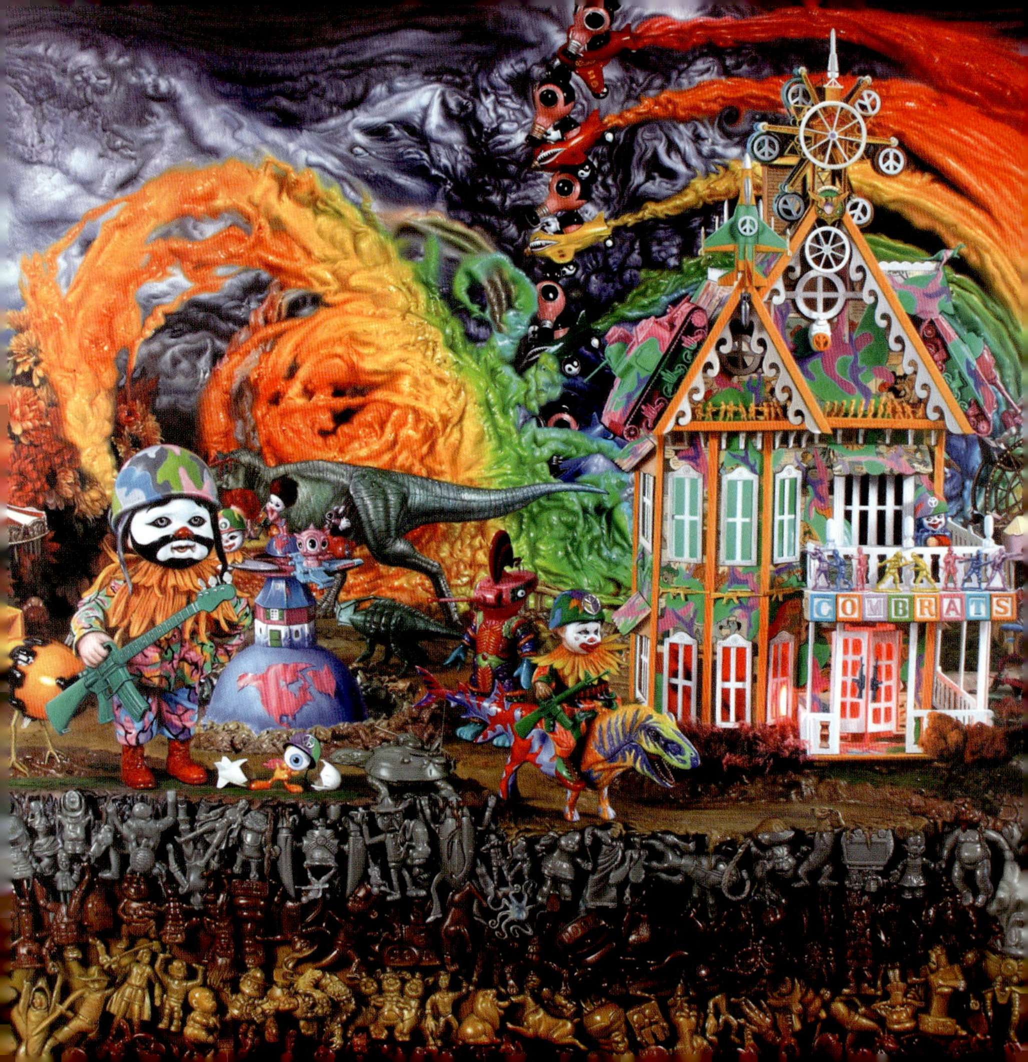
COMBRATS

I've built my house with the stones you've thrown.

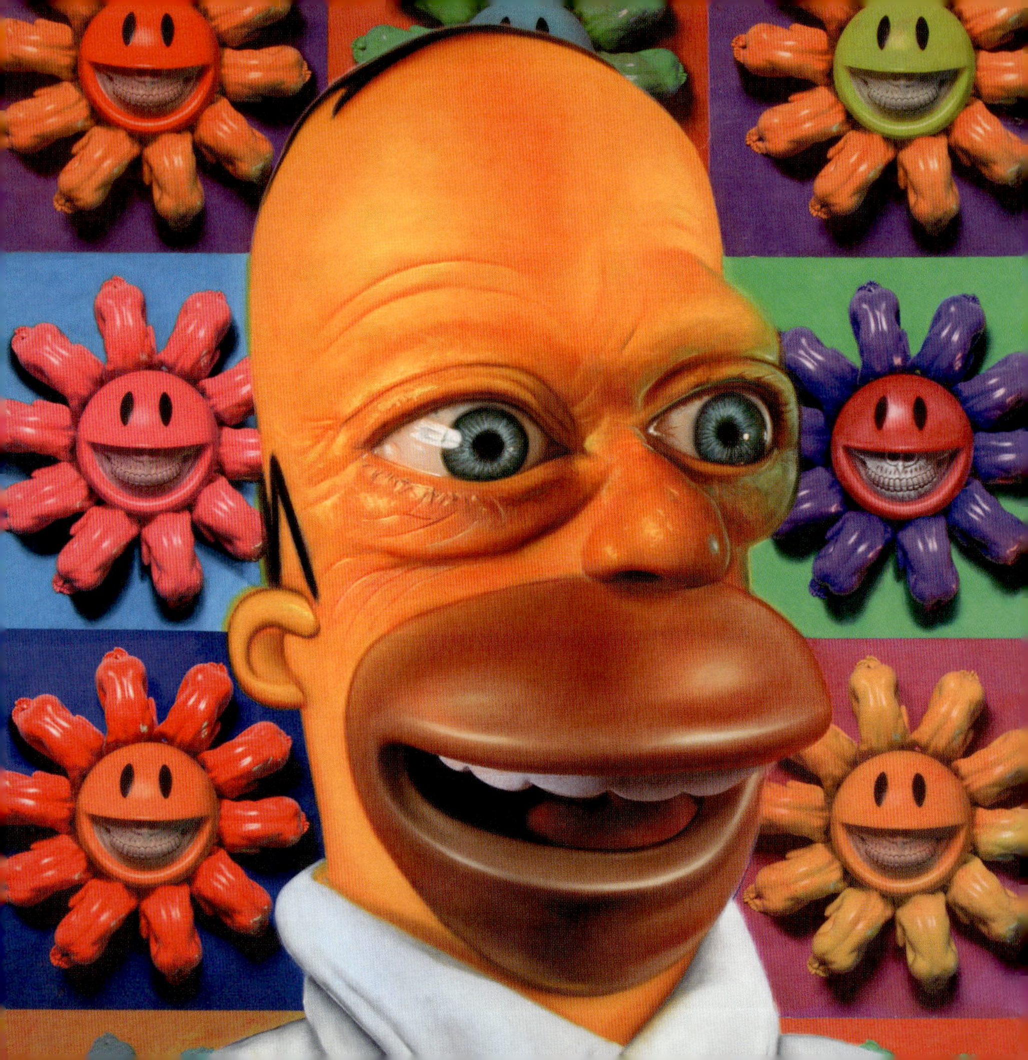

Life is hardest on the headstrong.

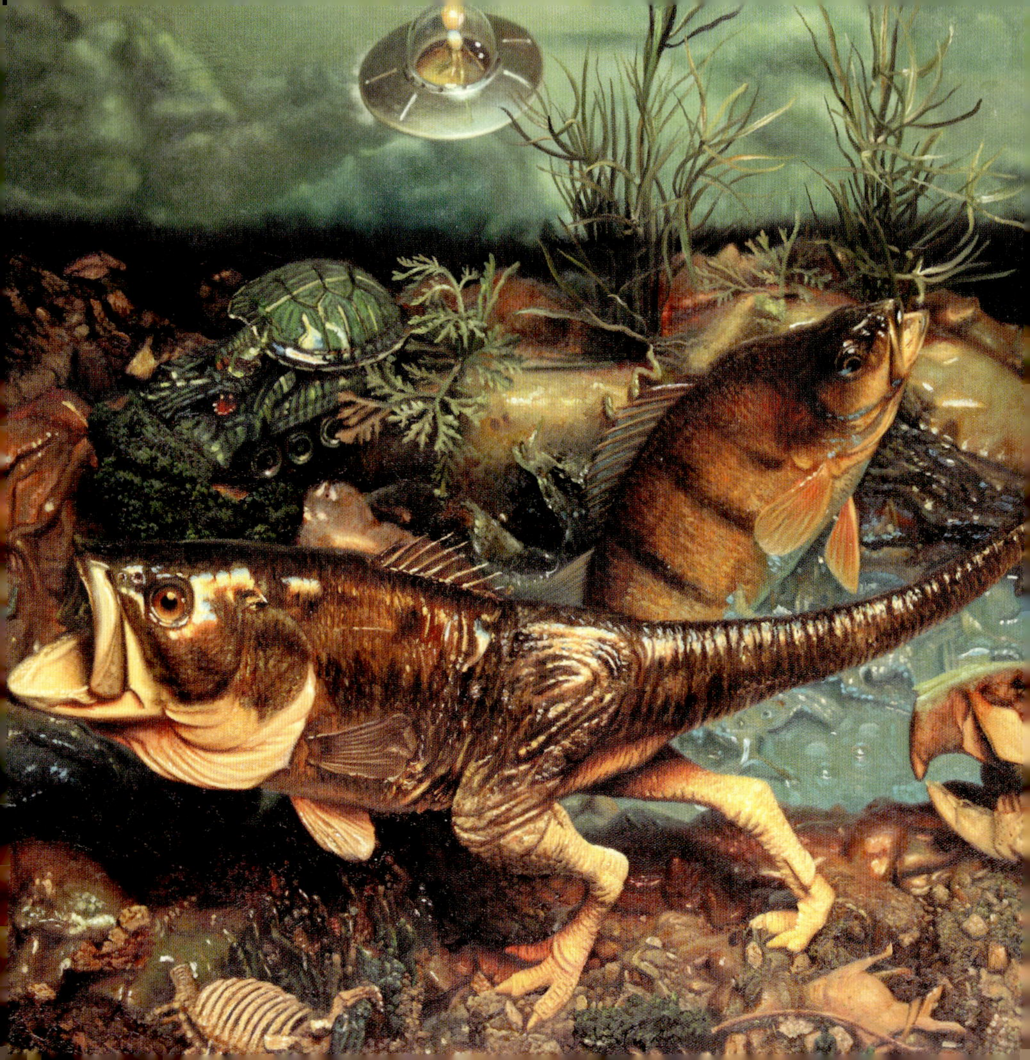

The fastest way to the future is to bypass the past.

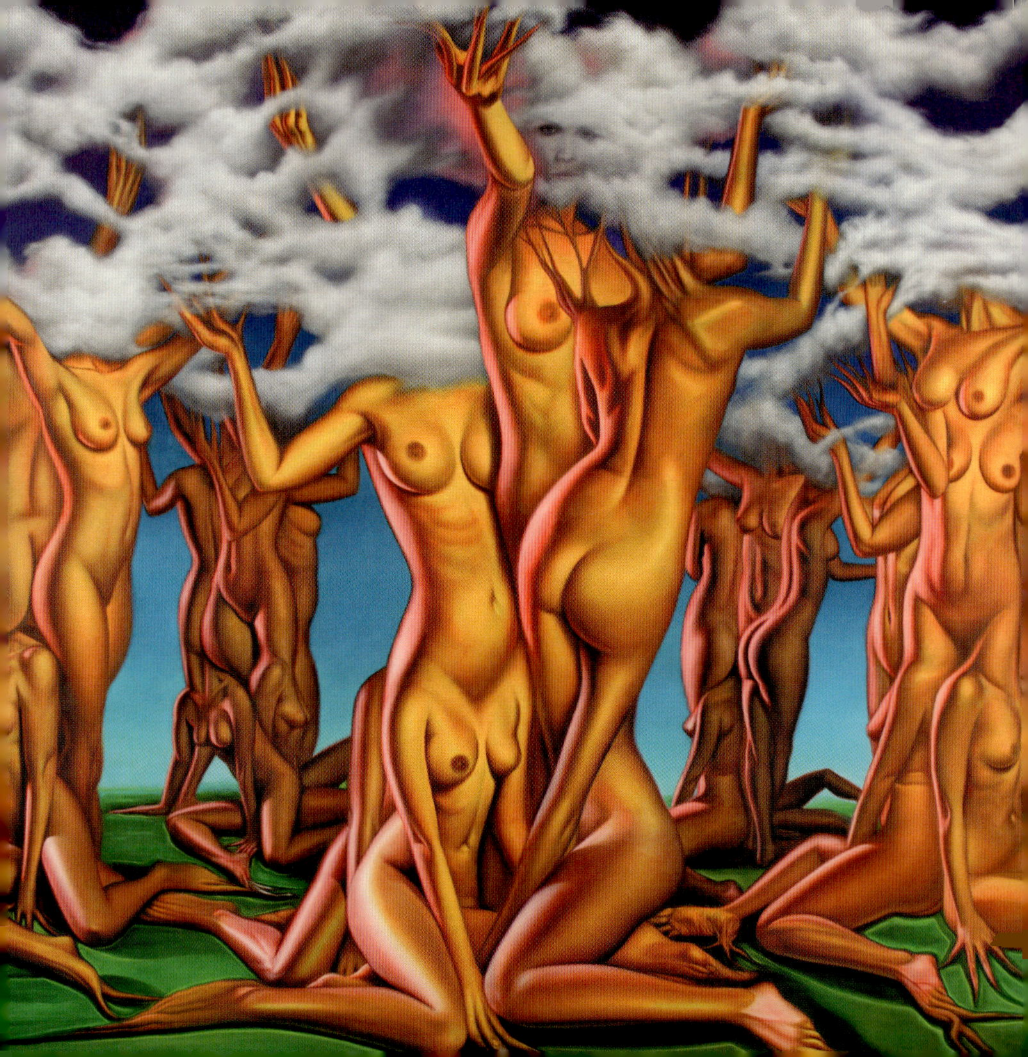

Every silver lining obscures a cloud.

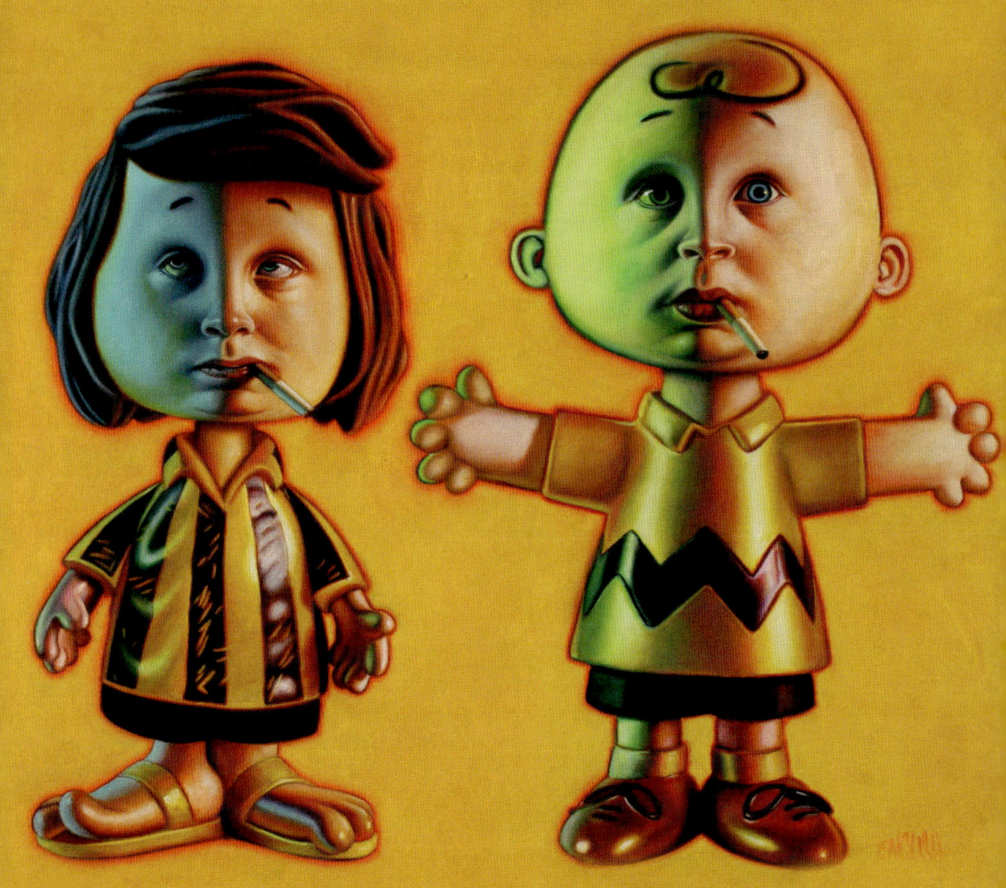

If I wanted your opinion, I wouldn’t bother having one of my own.

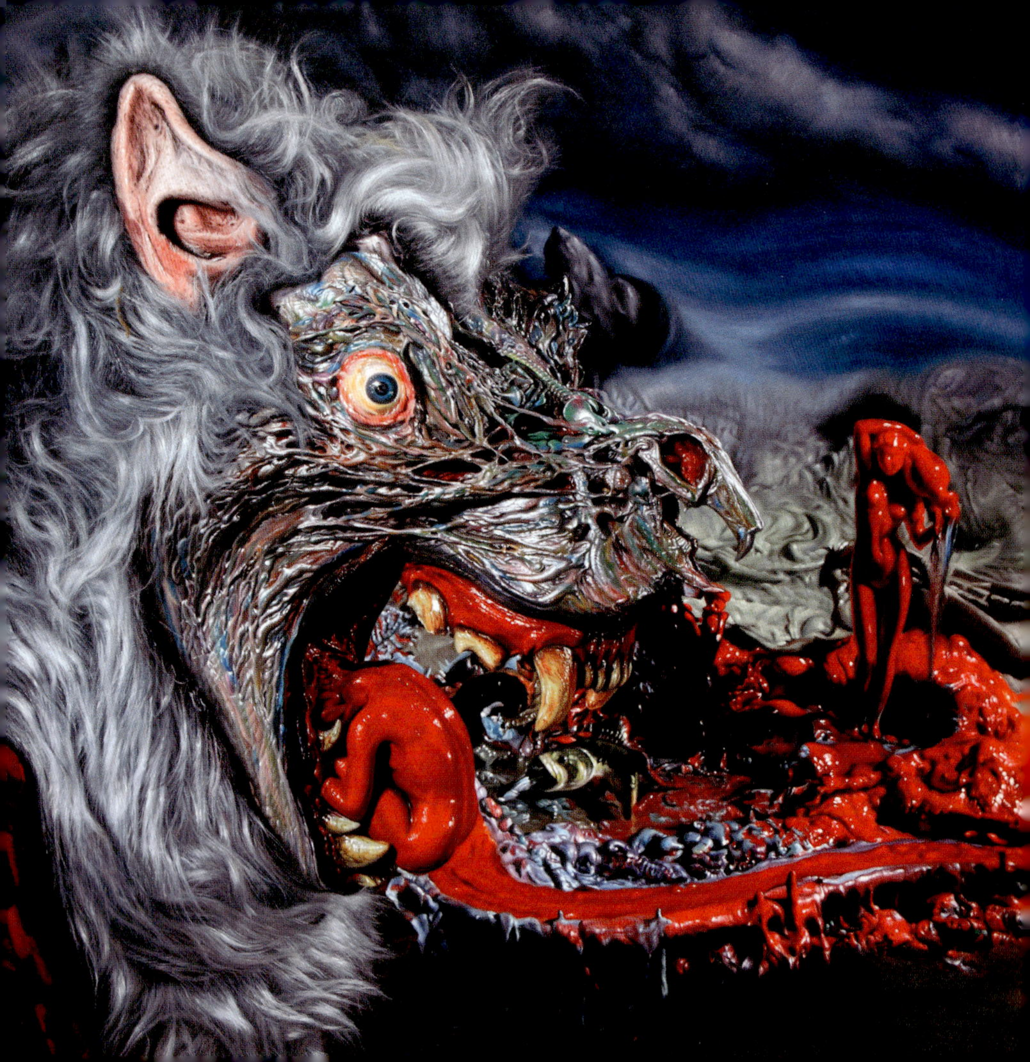

The best things in life have fleas.

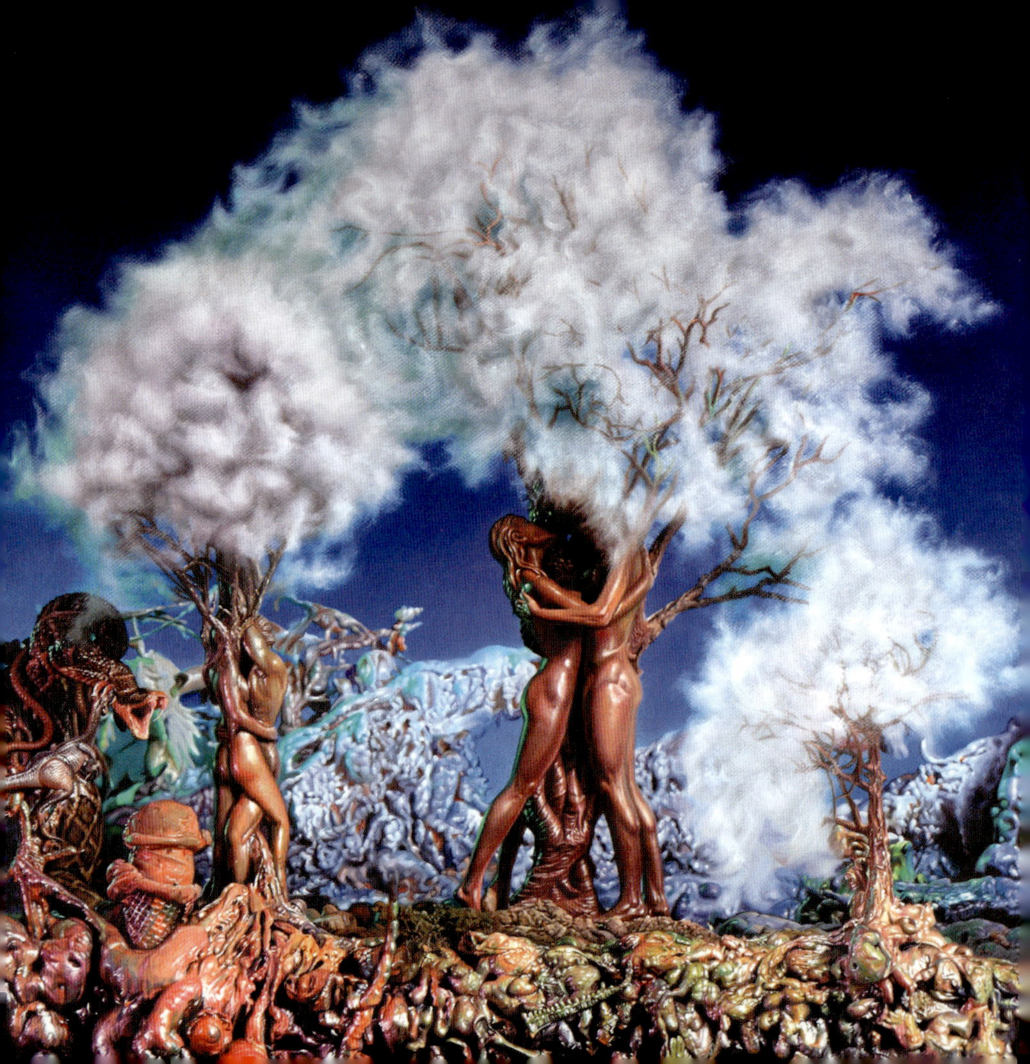

A ripe apple never toppled the tree.

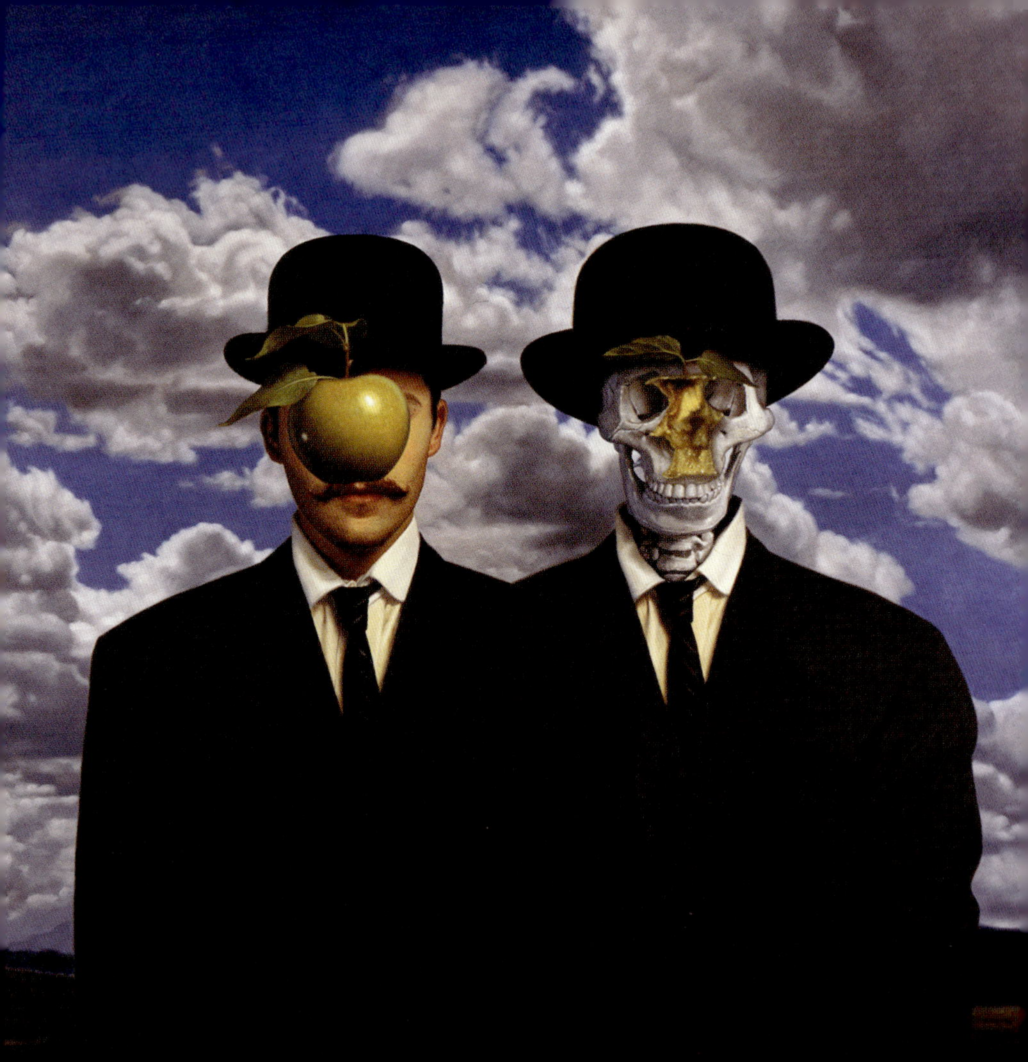

Patience is wasted on the lazy.

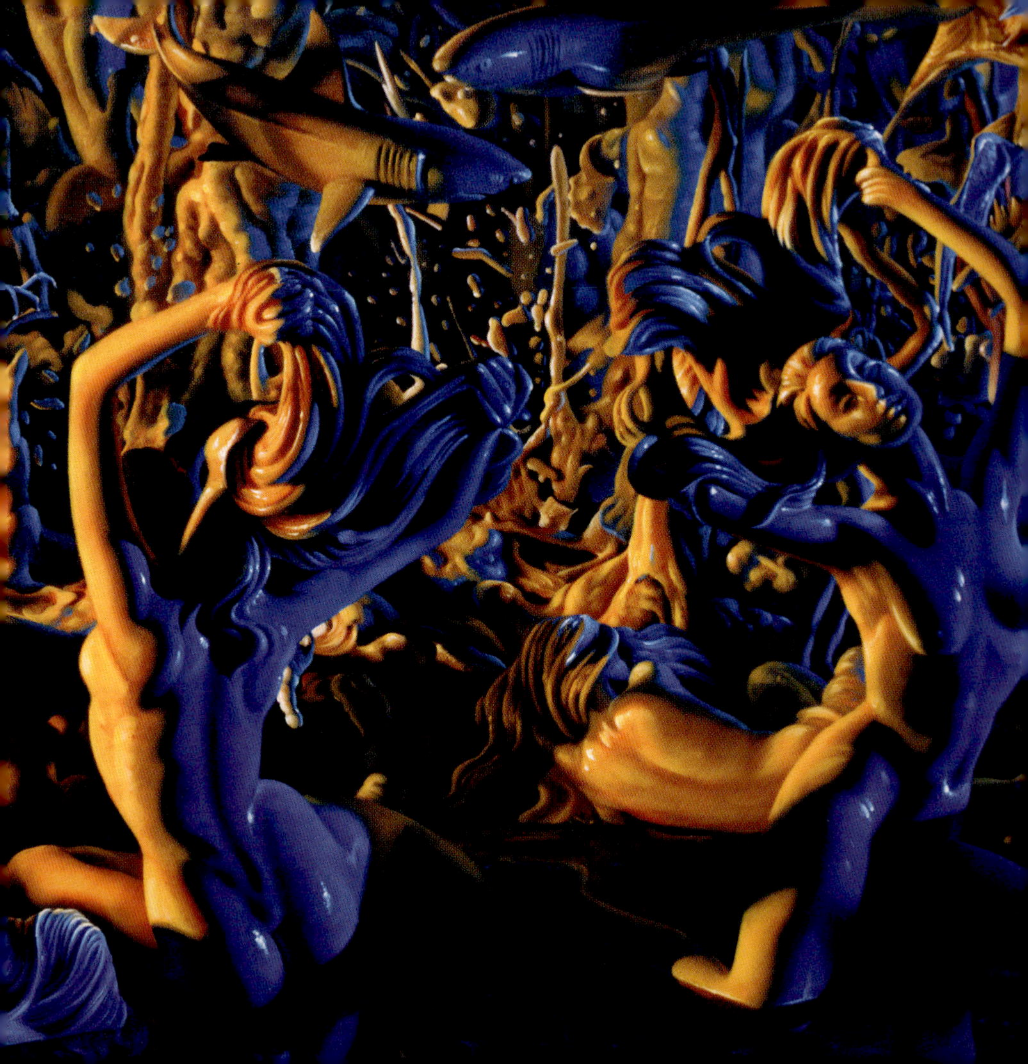

Every river is looking for an ocean.

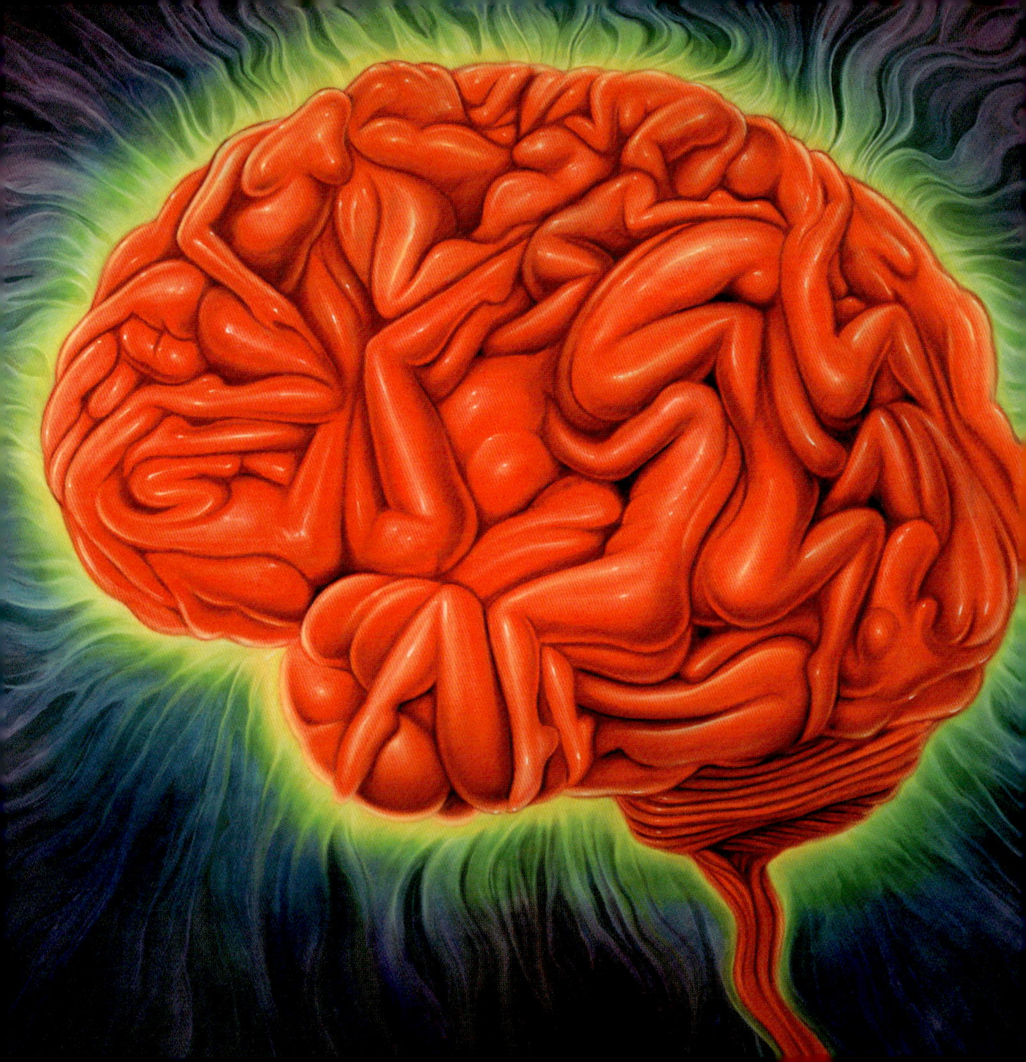

My thoughts hold my mind together.

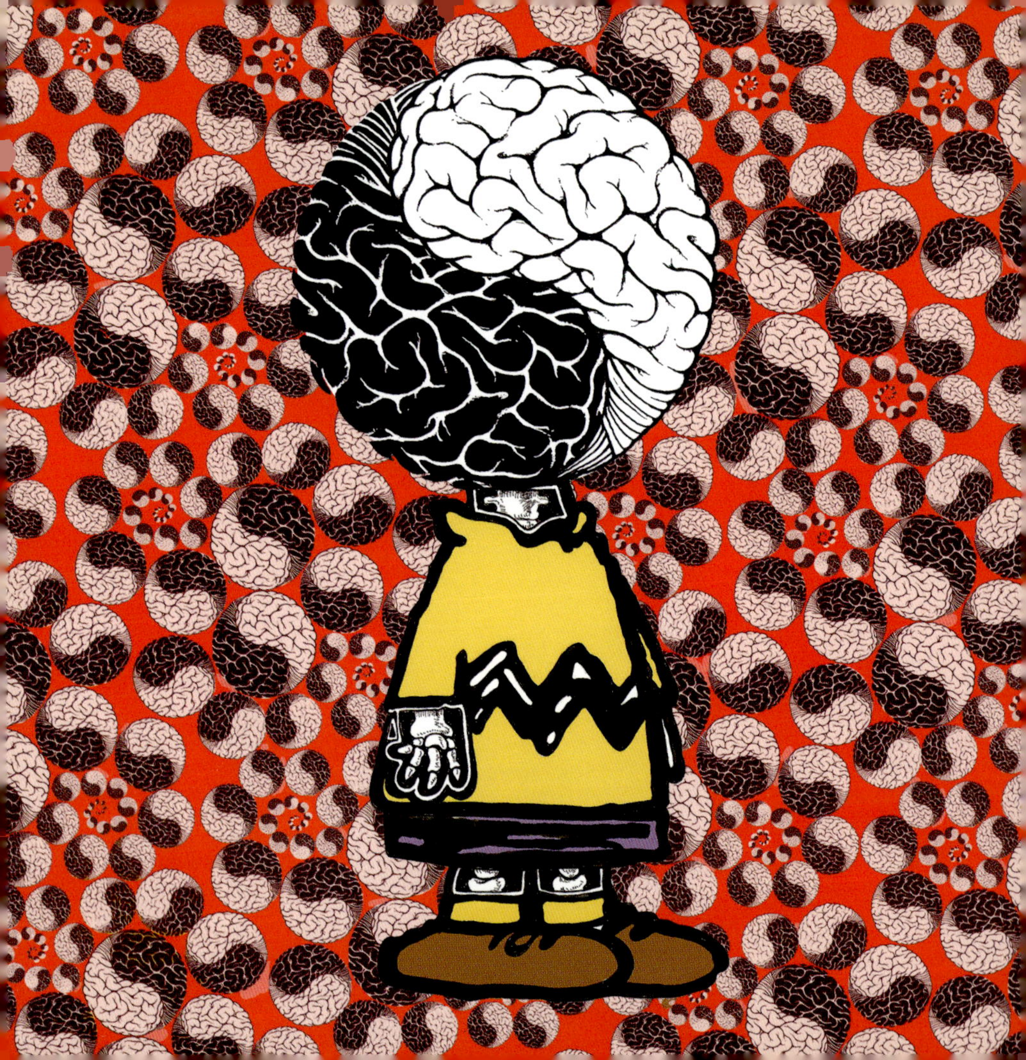

Holding contradictory ideas balances the brain.

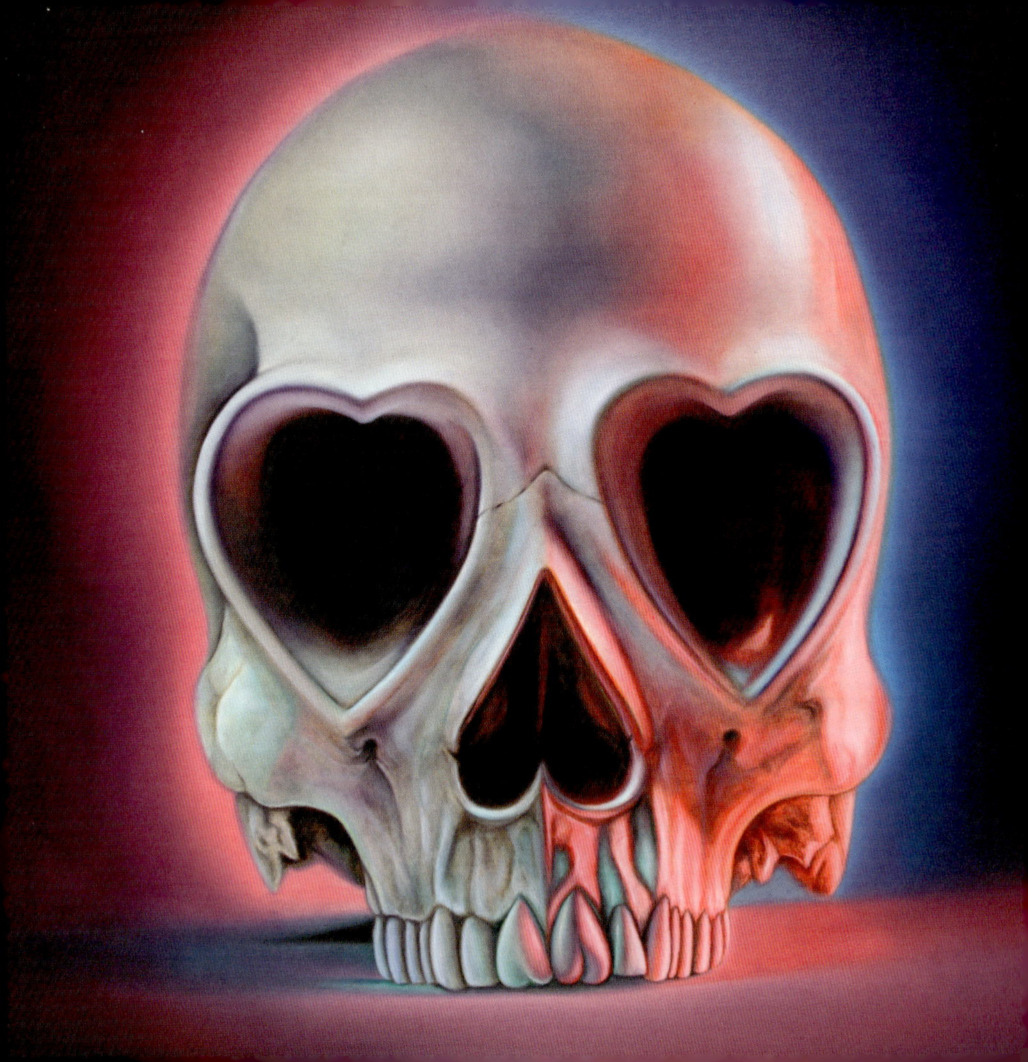

The human heart beats itself to death.

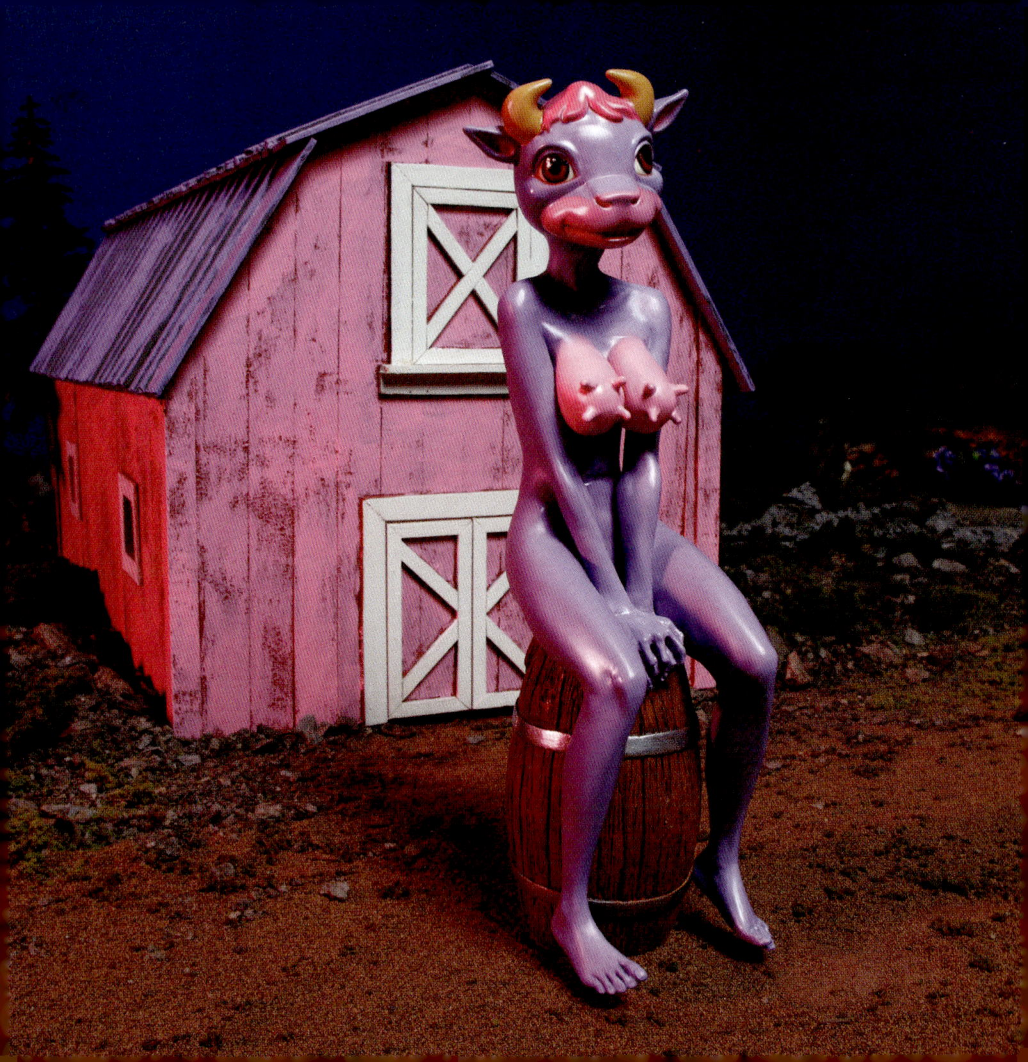

Nothing is normal until you get used to it.

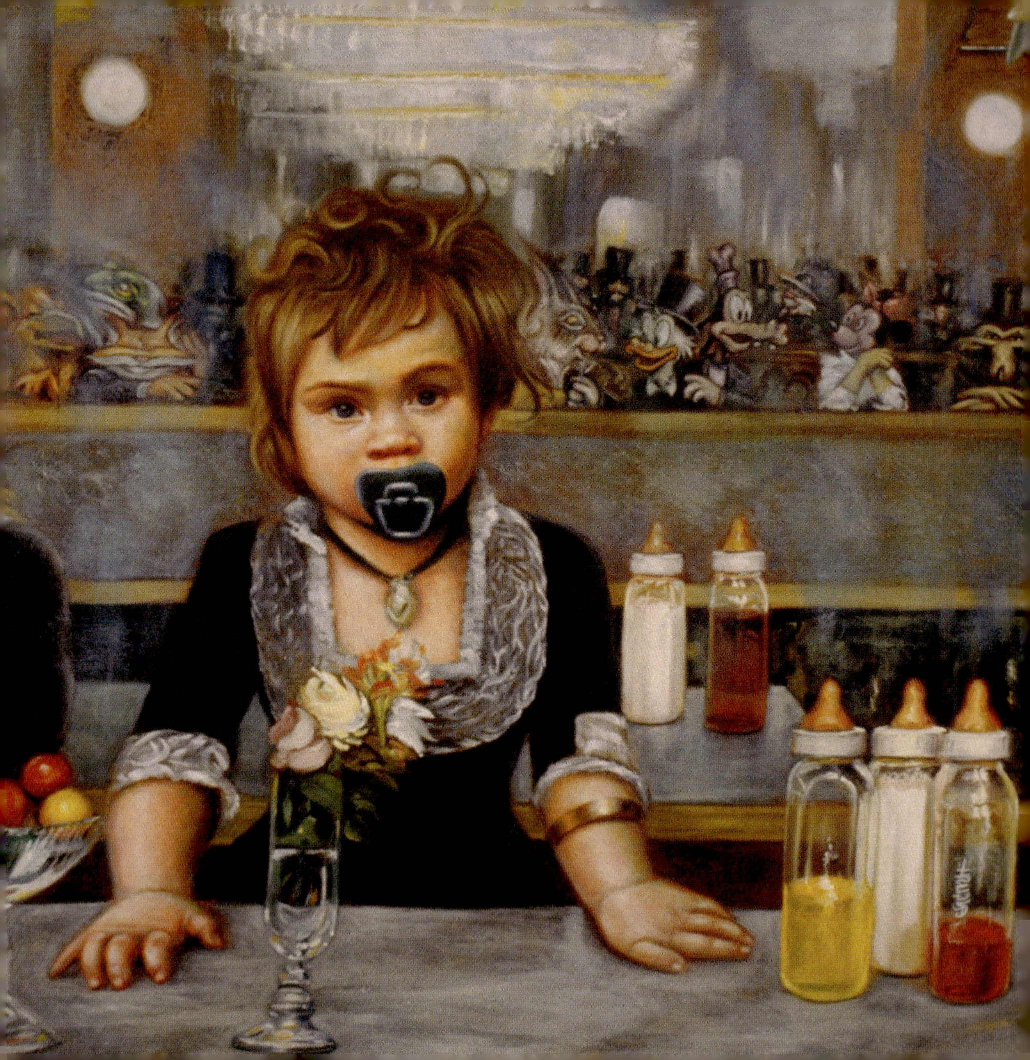

You're only young
forever.

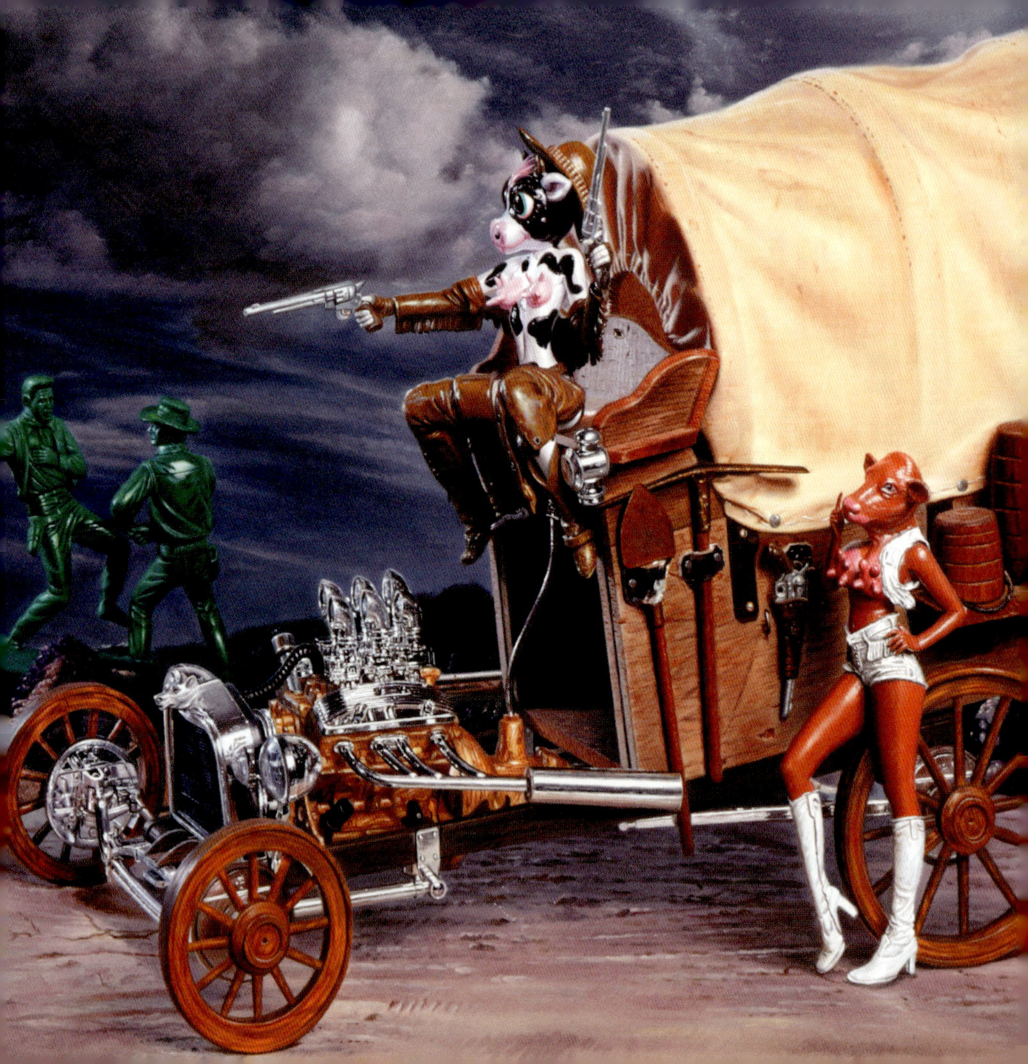

It's not the journey that weighs you down; it's the baggage.

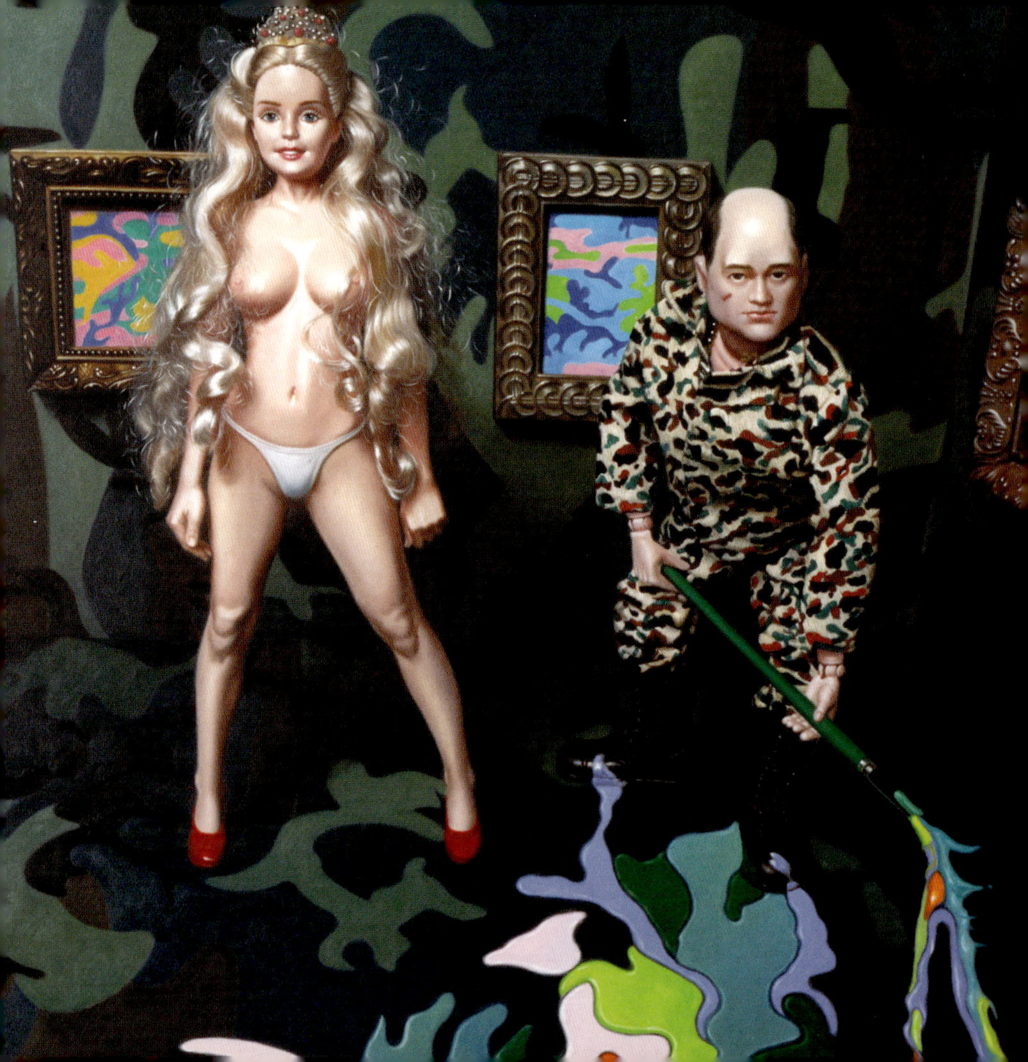

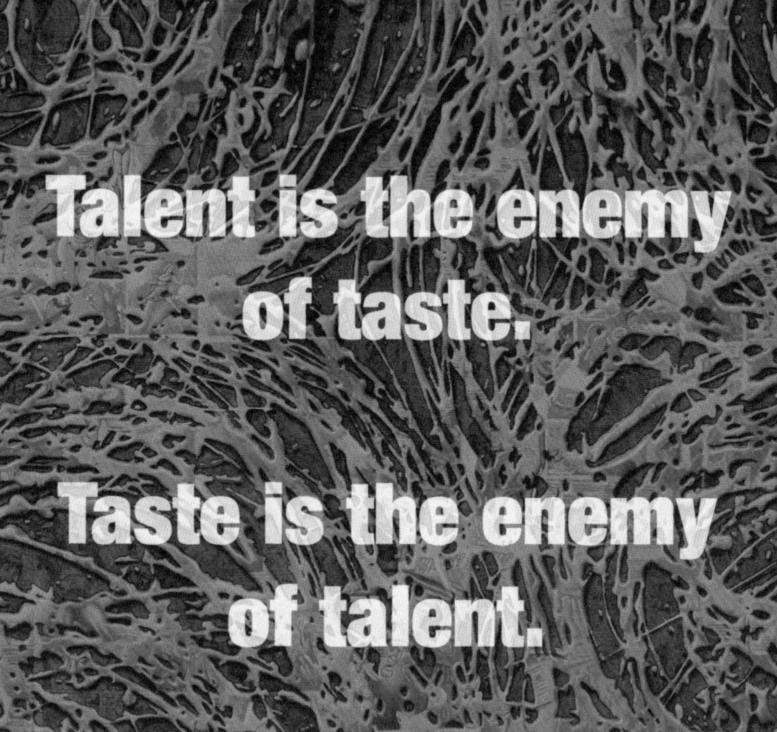
Talent is the enemy
of taste.
Taste is the enemy
of talent.

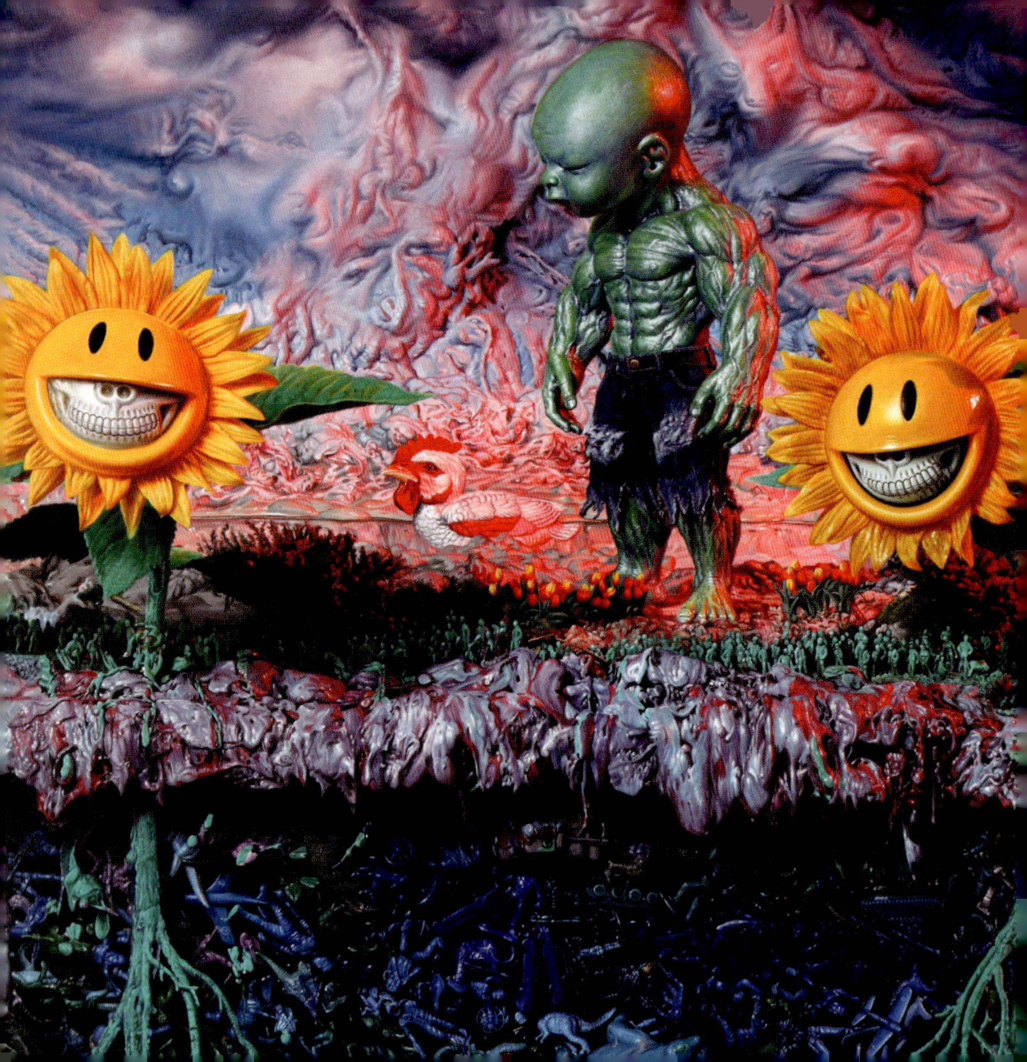

The longest journey
ends where
apathy begins.

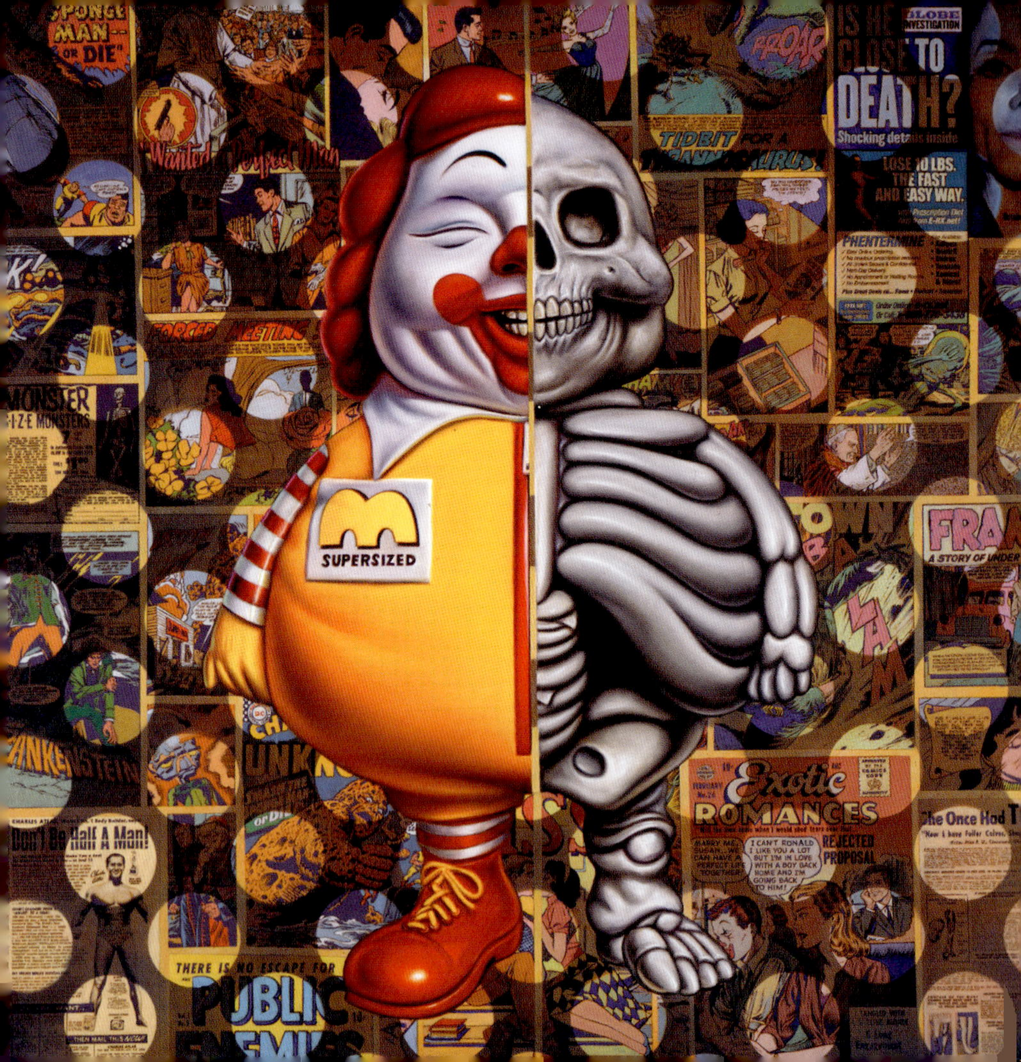

SPONGE MAN— OR DIE
ROAR
GLOBE INVESTIGATION
DEATH?
LOSE 10 LBS. THE FAST AND EASY WAY.
PHENTERMINE
FORCED MEETING
MONSTER
S-I-Z-E MONSTERS
SUPERSIZED
A STORY OF UNDER
Exotic ROMANCES
REJECTED PROPOSAL
I CAN'T RONALD I LIKE YOU A LOT BUT I'M IN LOVE WITH A BOY BACK HOME AND I'M GOING BACK TO HIM!
Don't Be Half A Man!
THERE IS NO ESCAPE FOR
PUBLIC

You can't have your cake and your waistline too.

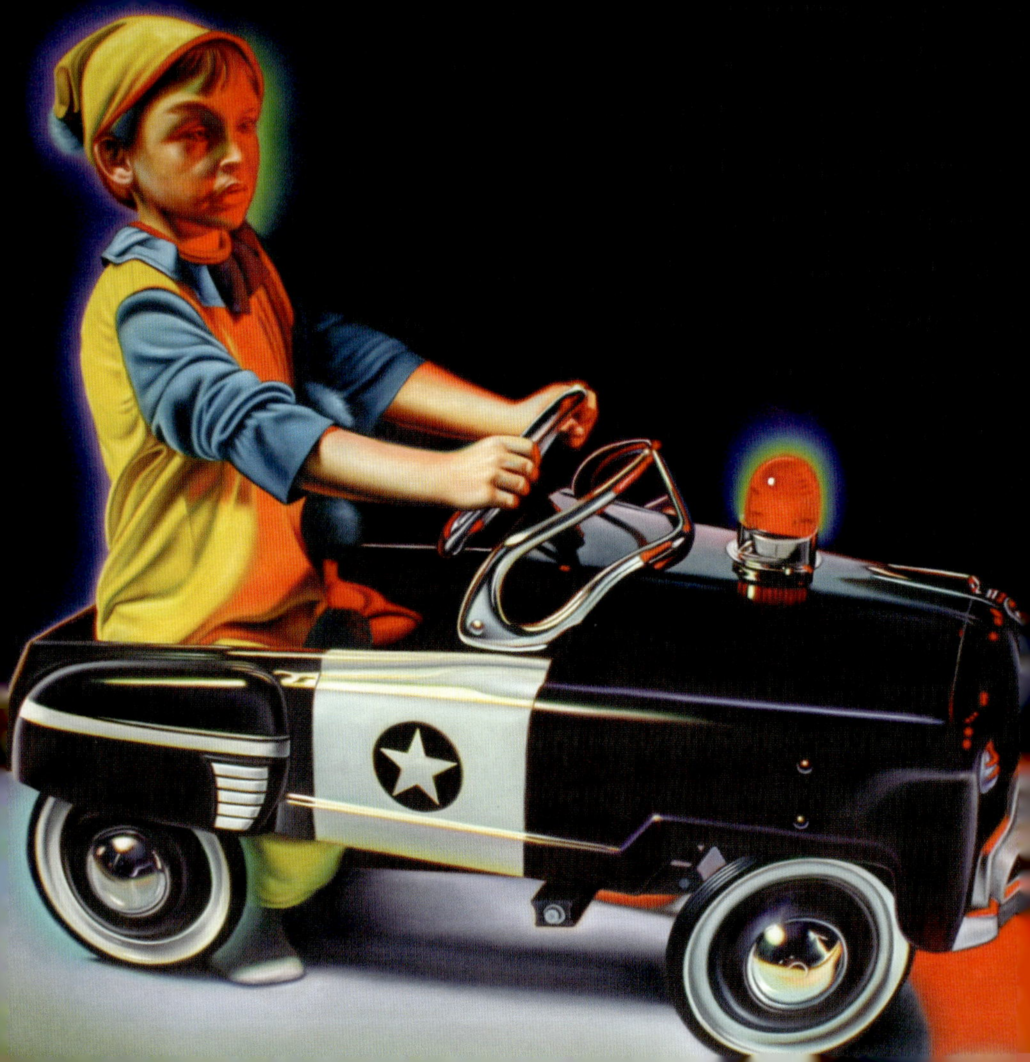

I'll stay awake
while reason sleeps.

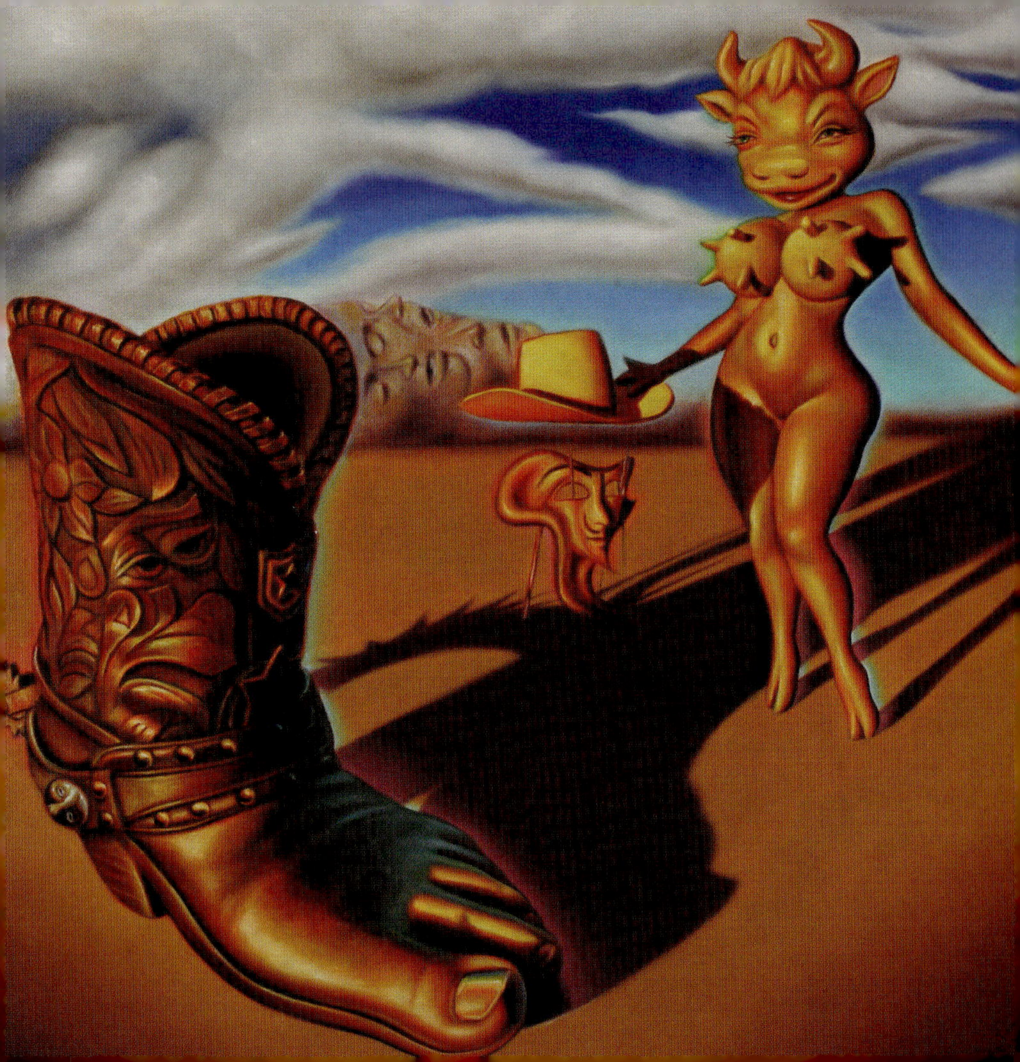

Memories forever remake the past.

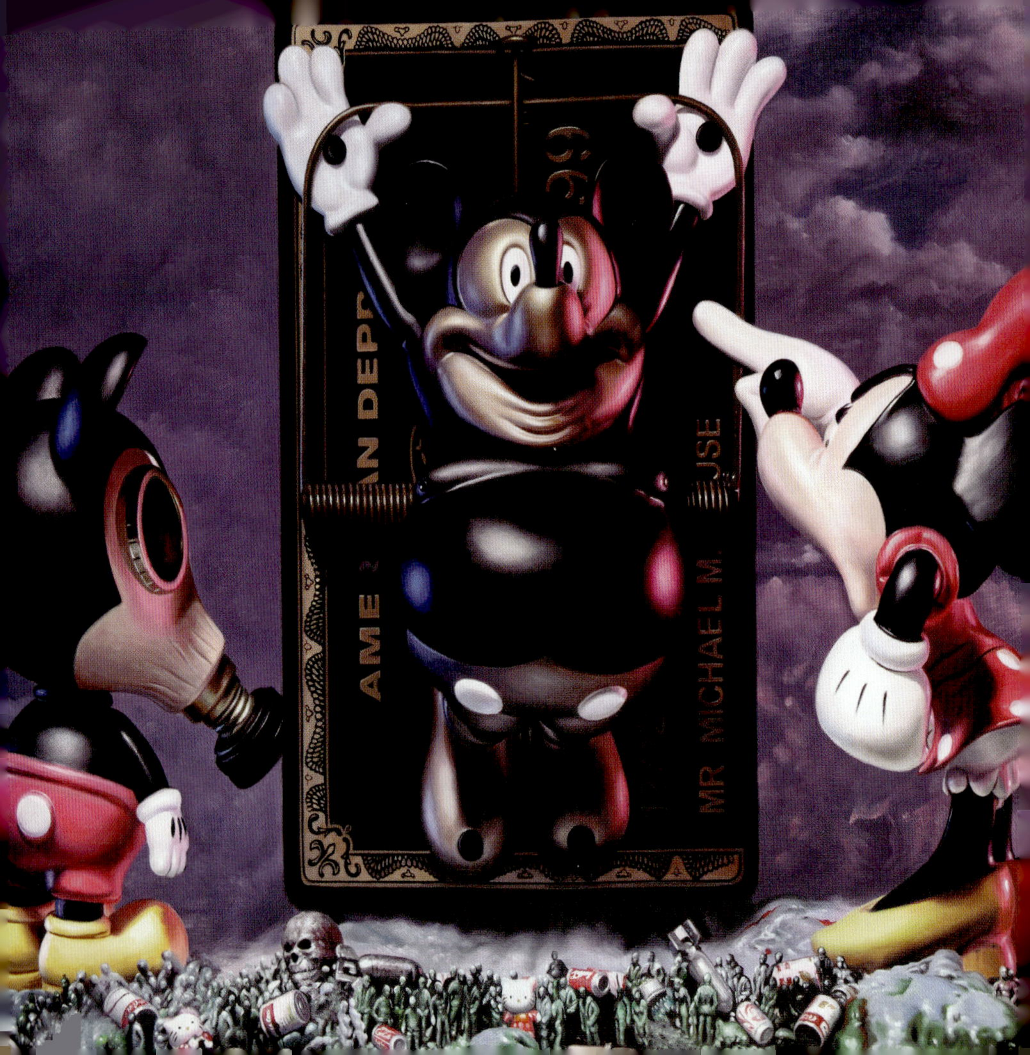
AME
AN DEPP
MR MICHAEL M.
USE

He who laughs last may be the joke.

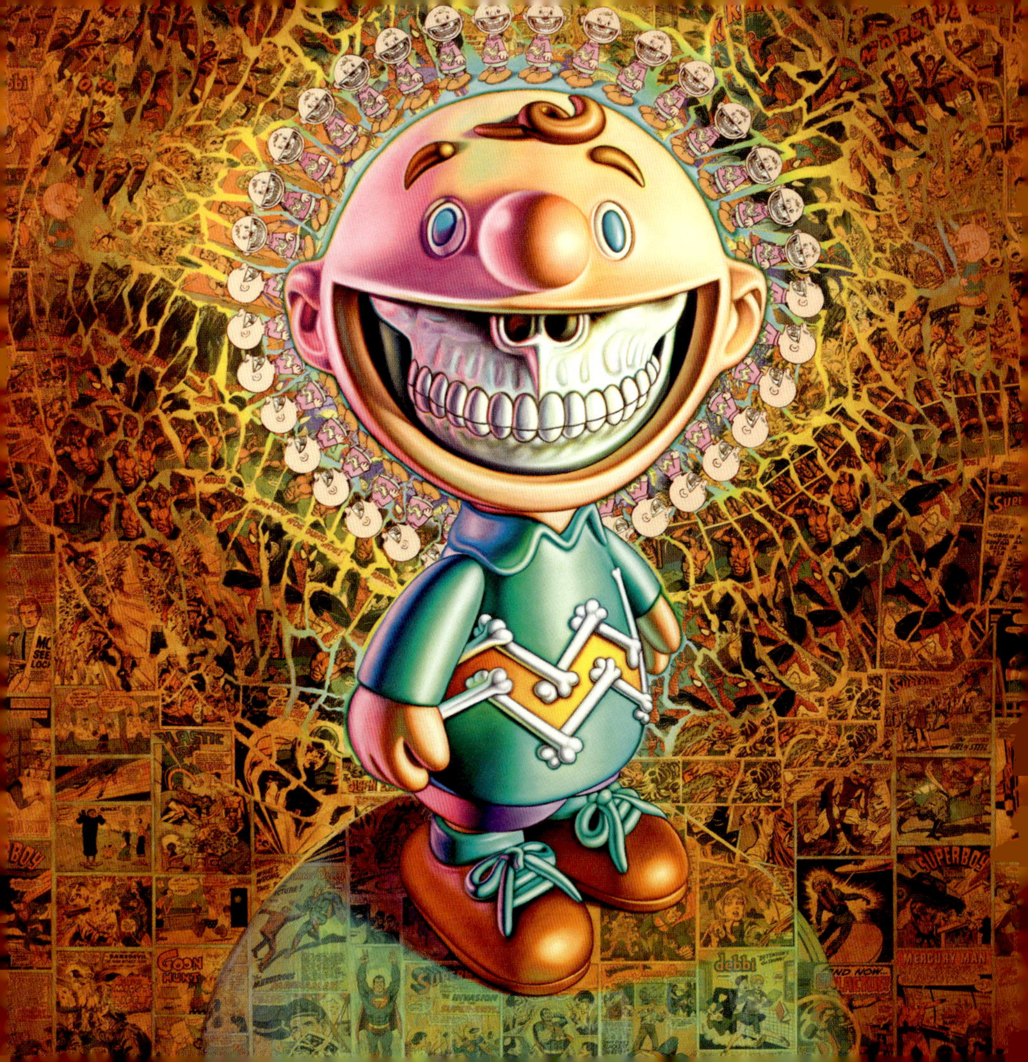
SUPERBOY
MERCURY MAN

He who laughs last didn't get the joke.

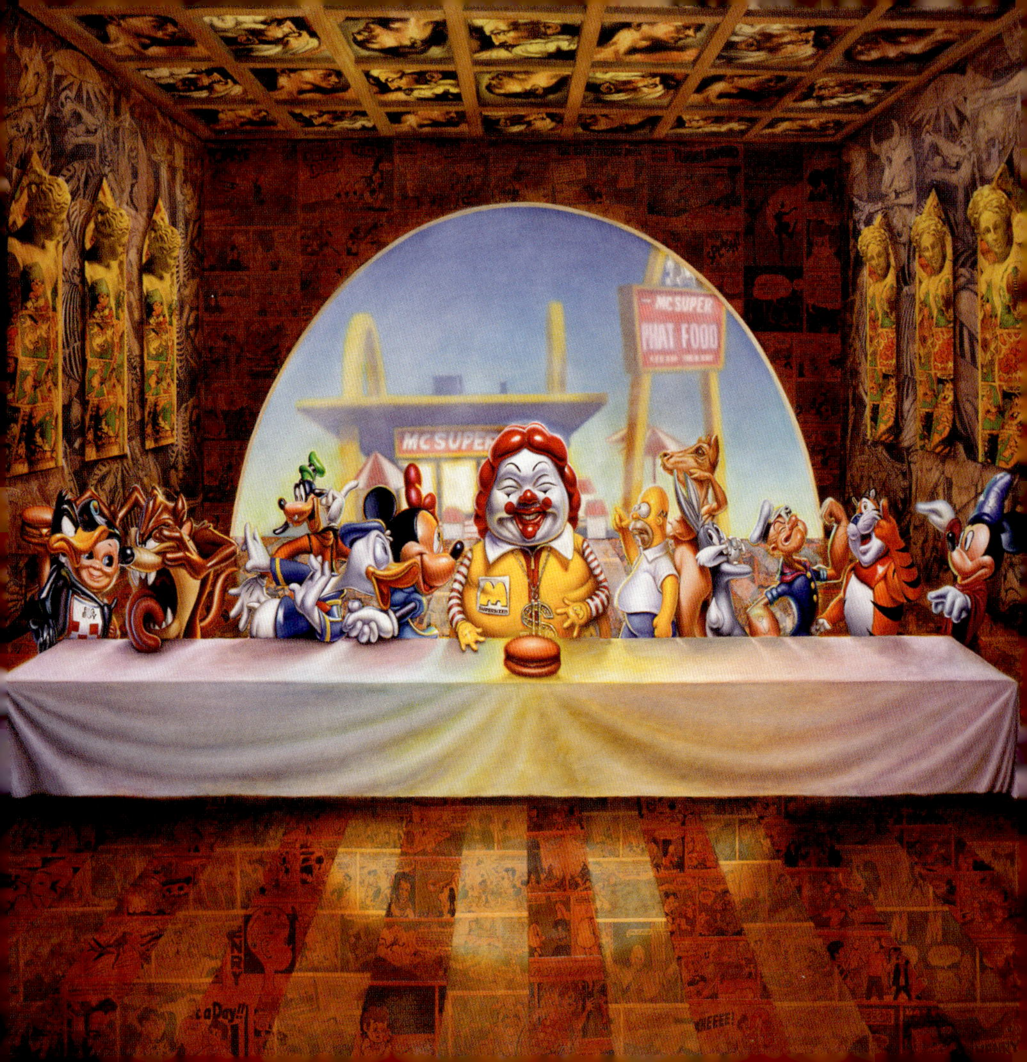
MC SUPER
PHAT FOOD
MC SUPER

Question, believe, or lose your mind.

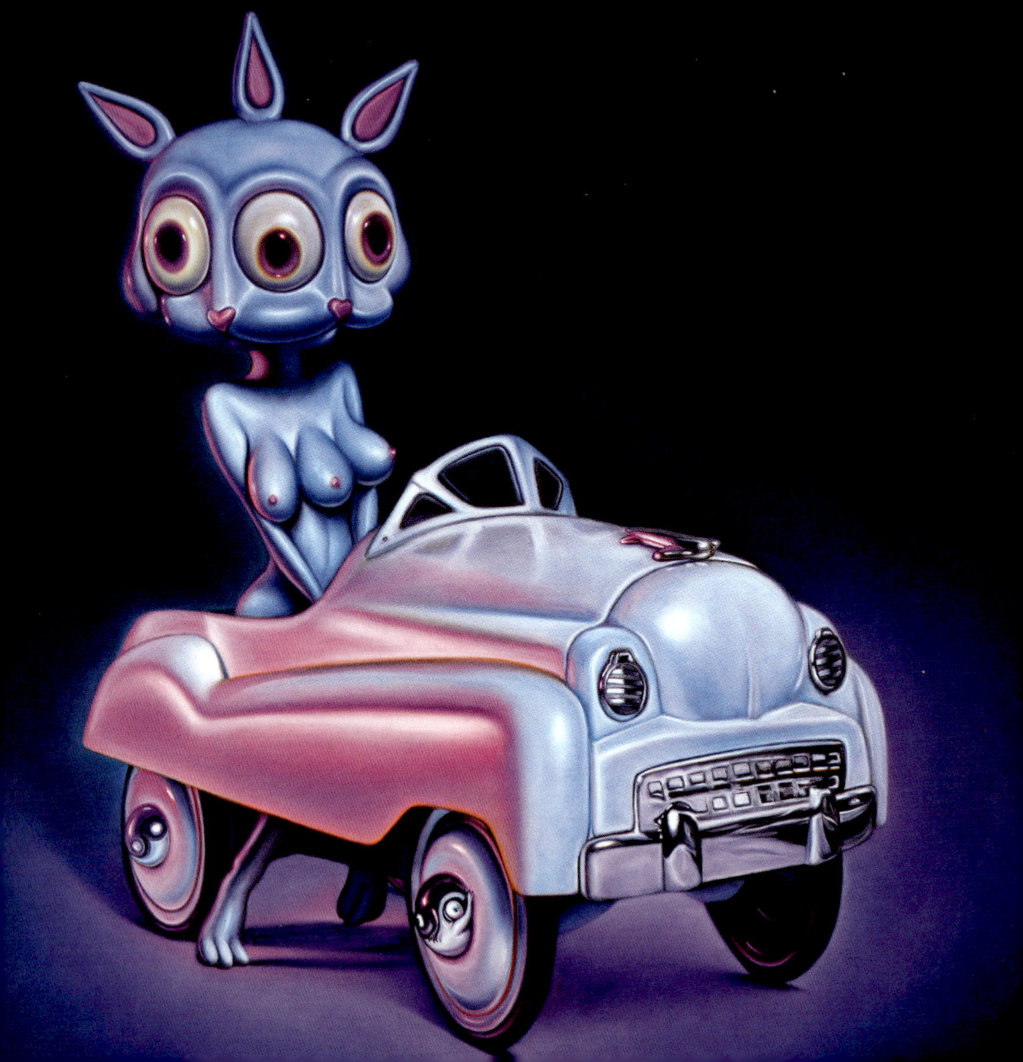

Two wrongs don't make a right, but three lefts do.

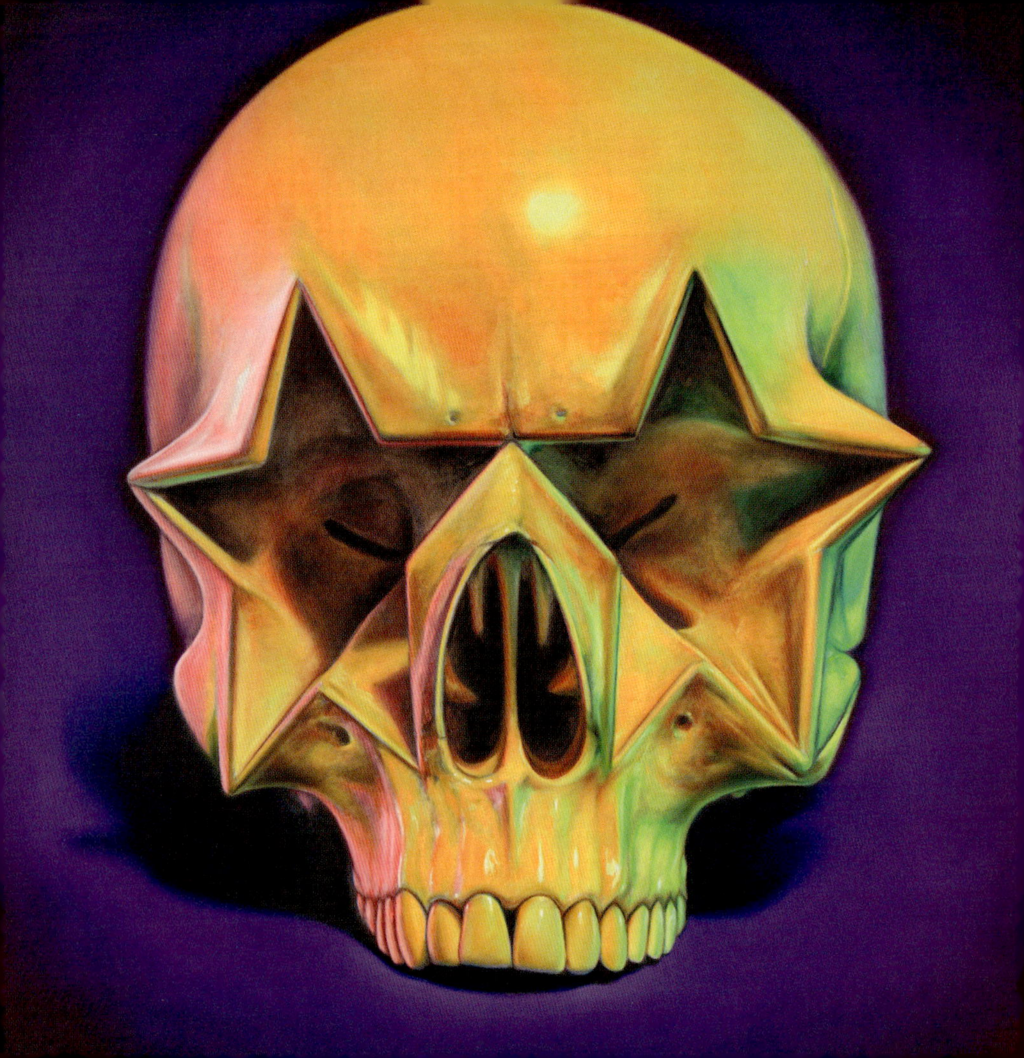

You may know
you're going to die,
but you won't know
you're dead.

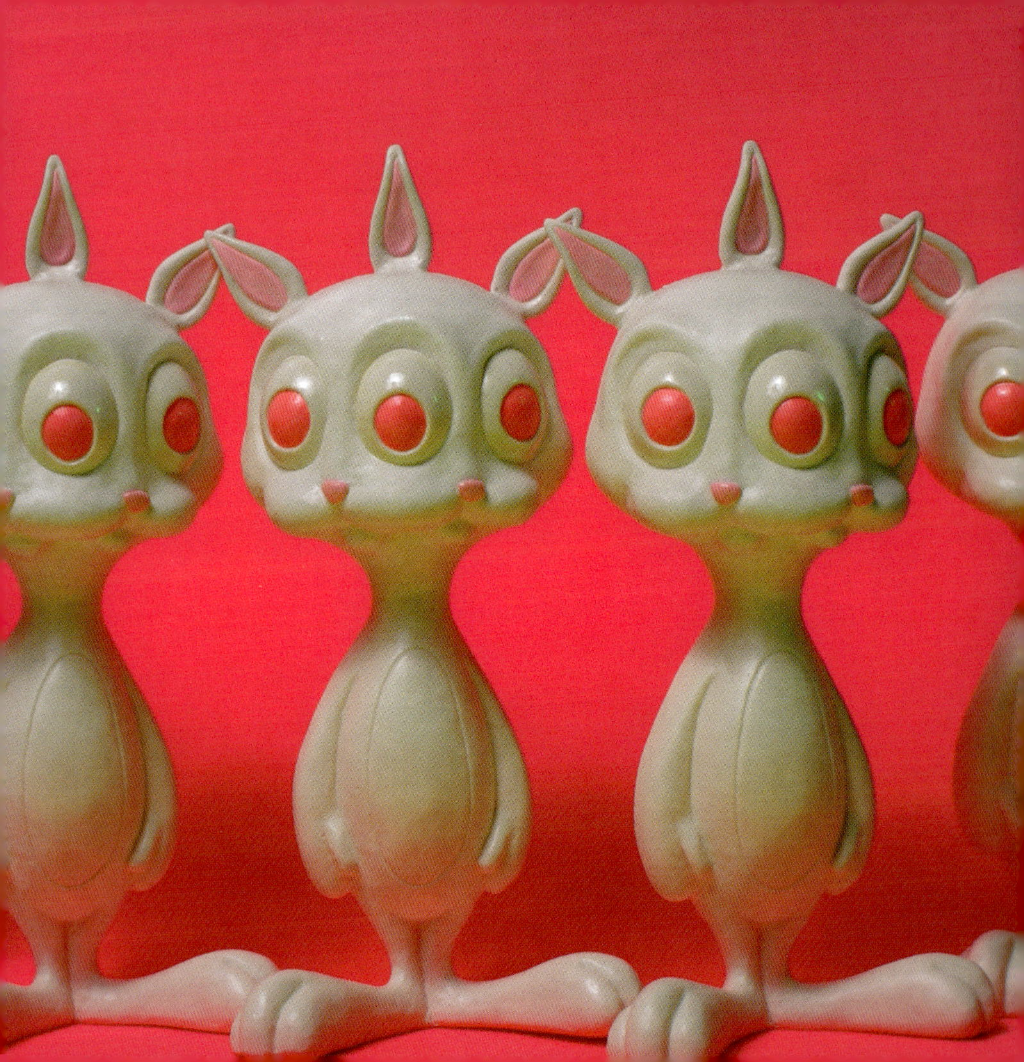

You are not a clone.

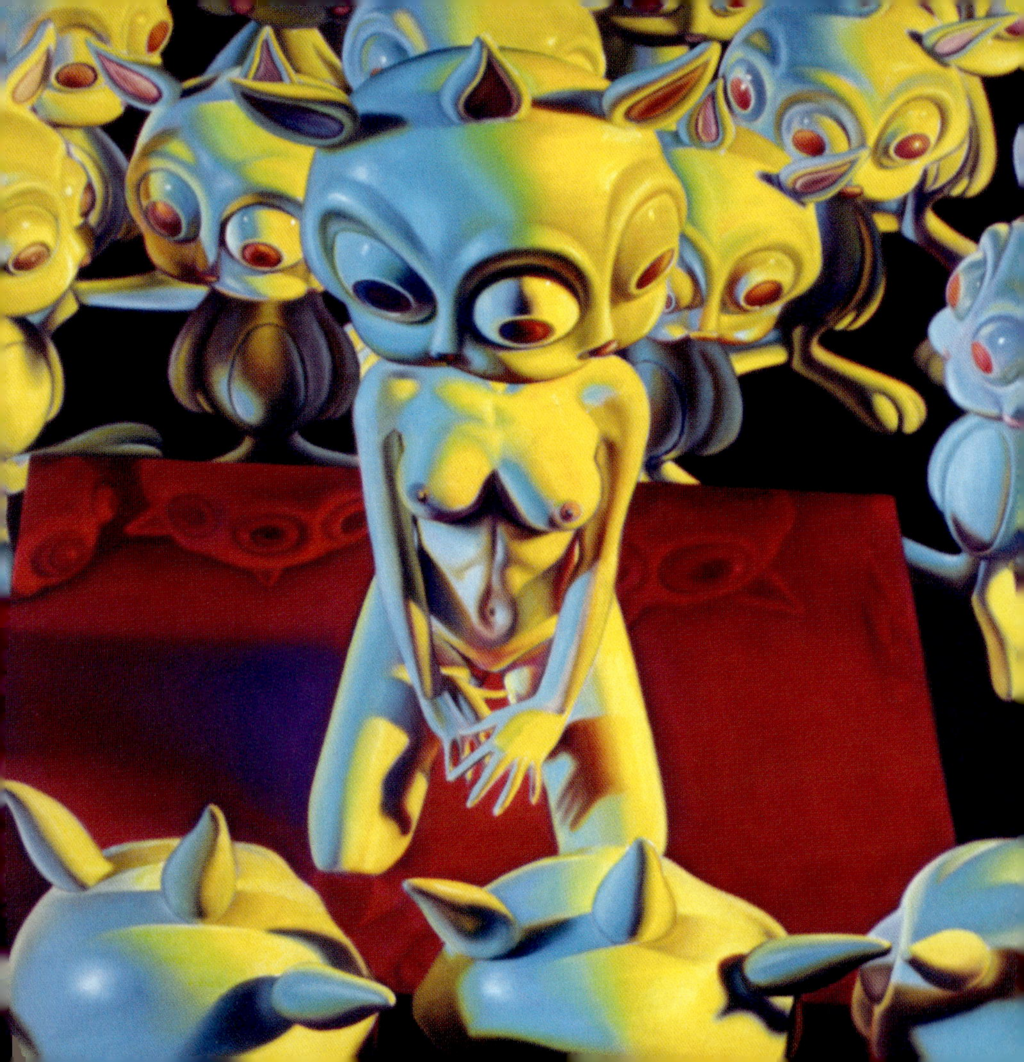

We are the new they.

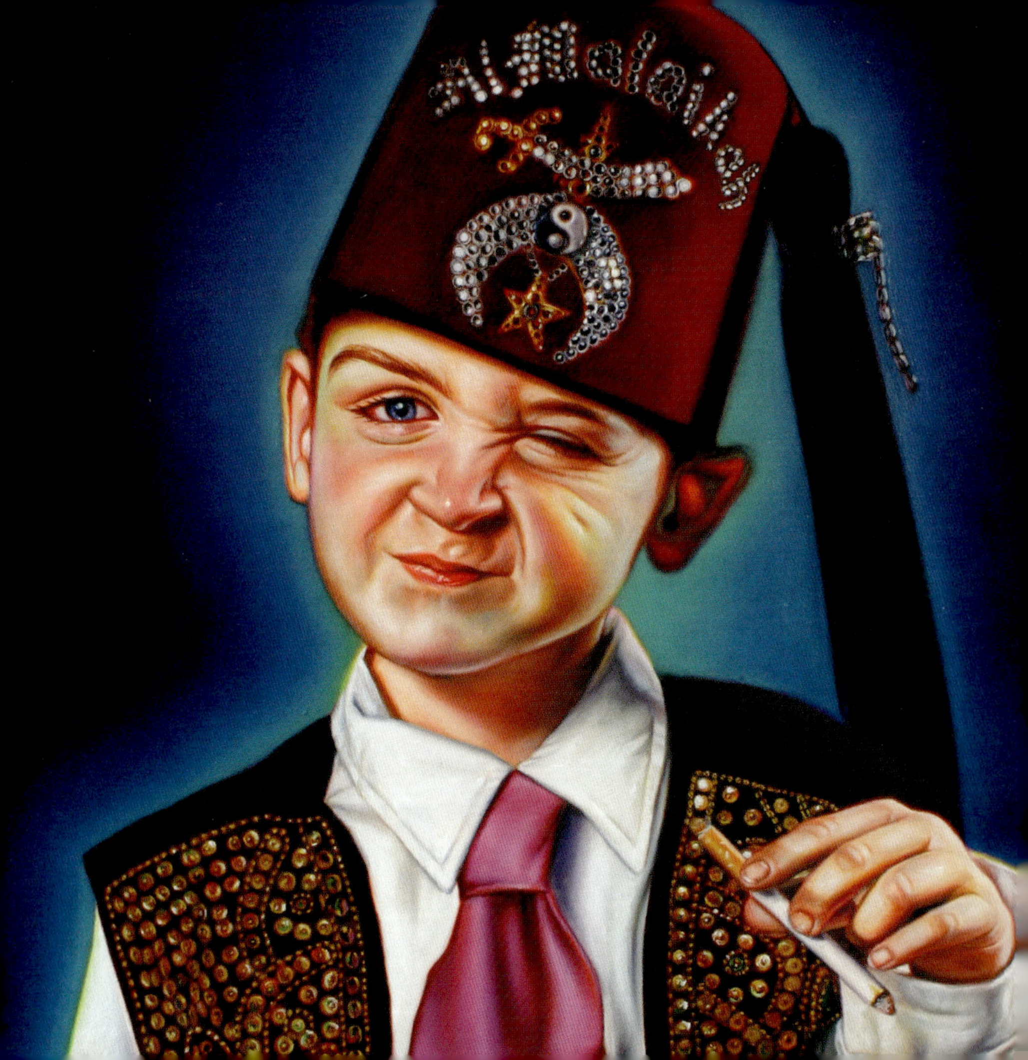

The lesser of two evils is not the greater good.

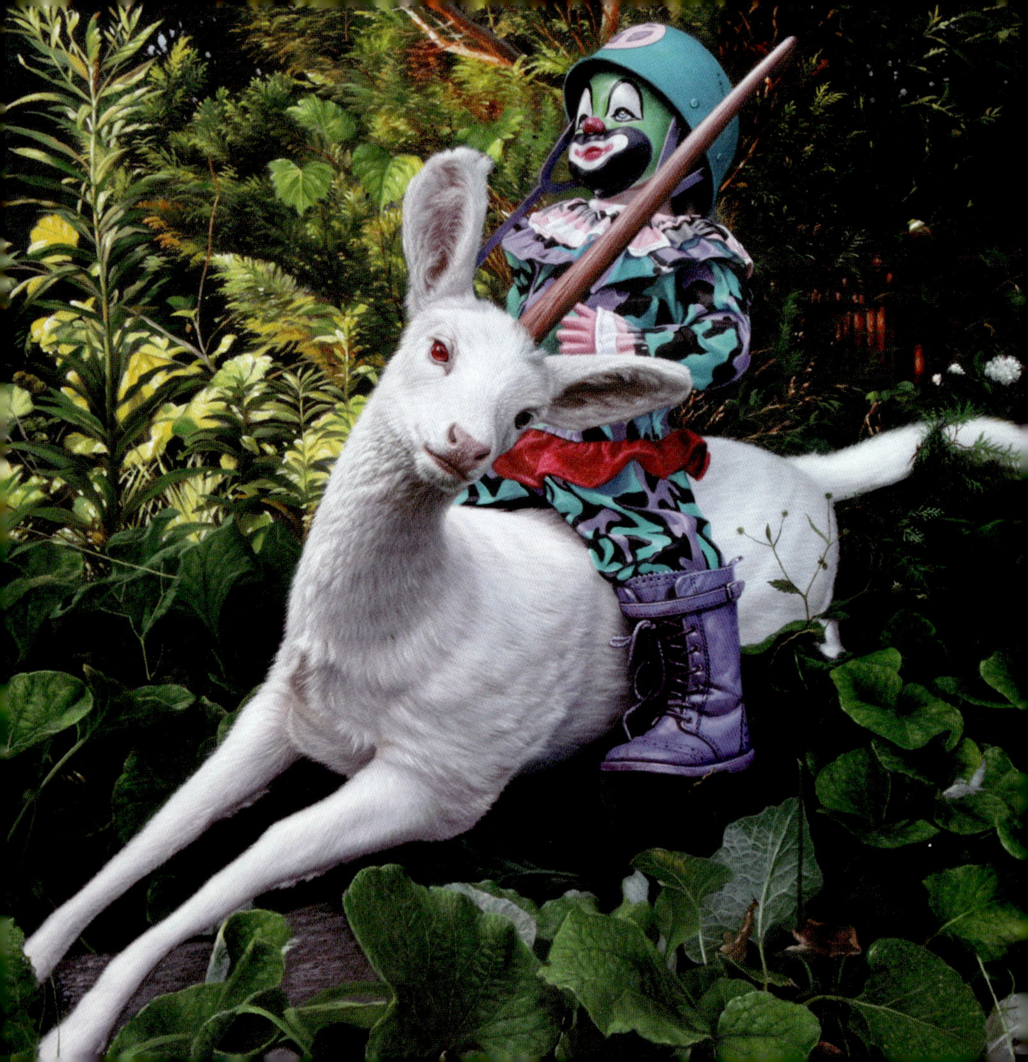

Evolution's the gift that keeps on giving.

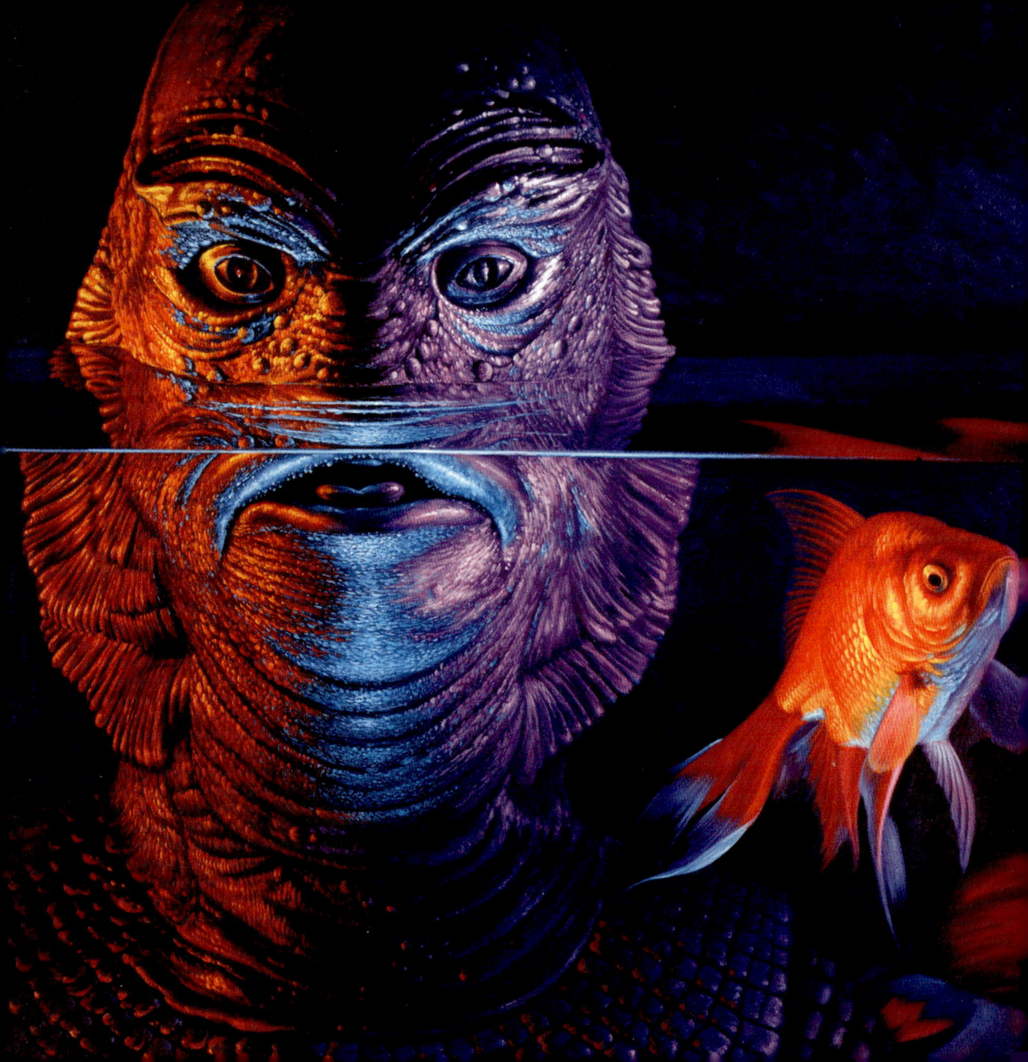

I may be shallow, but my thoughts are deep.

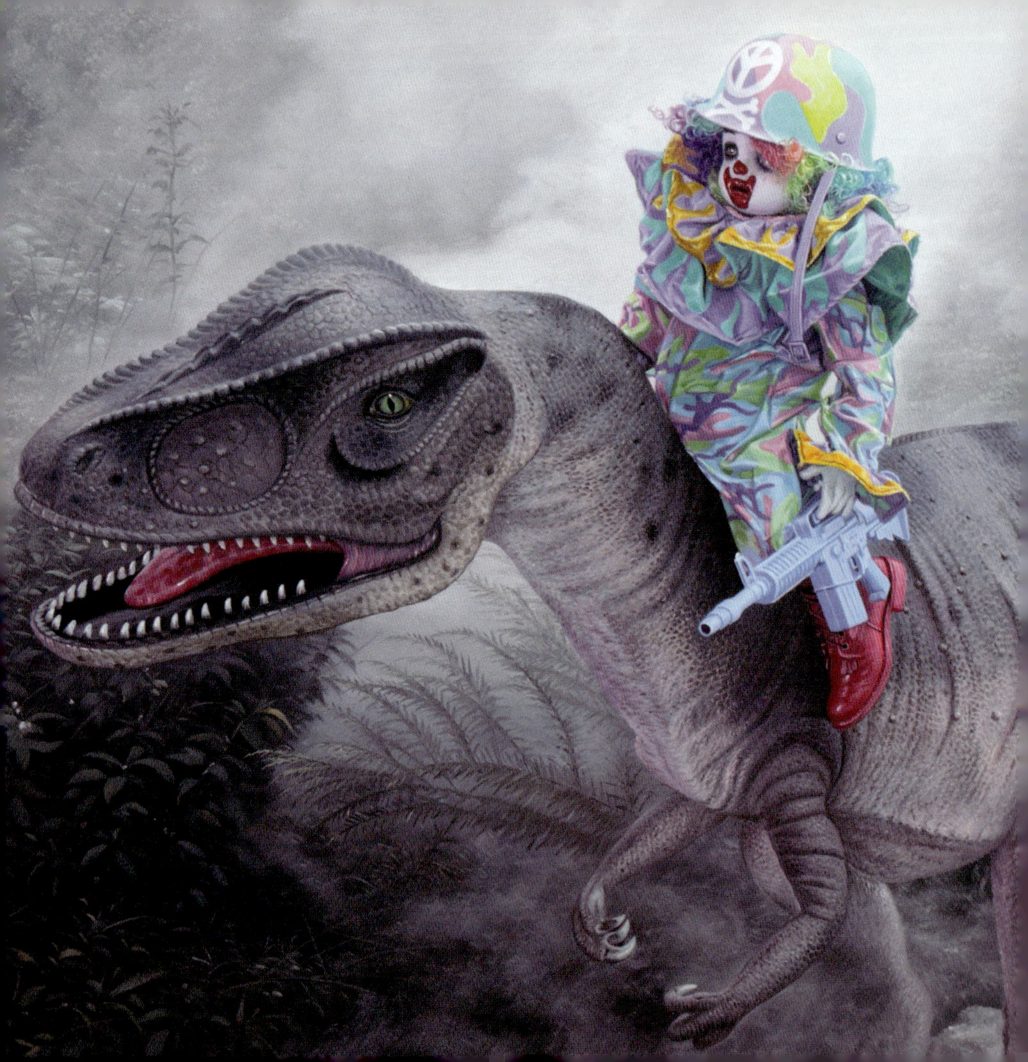

Pacifists lose the war; aggressors lose the peace.

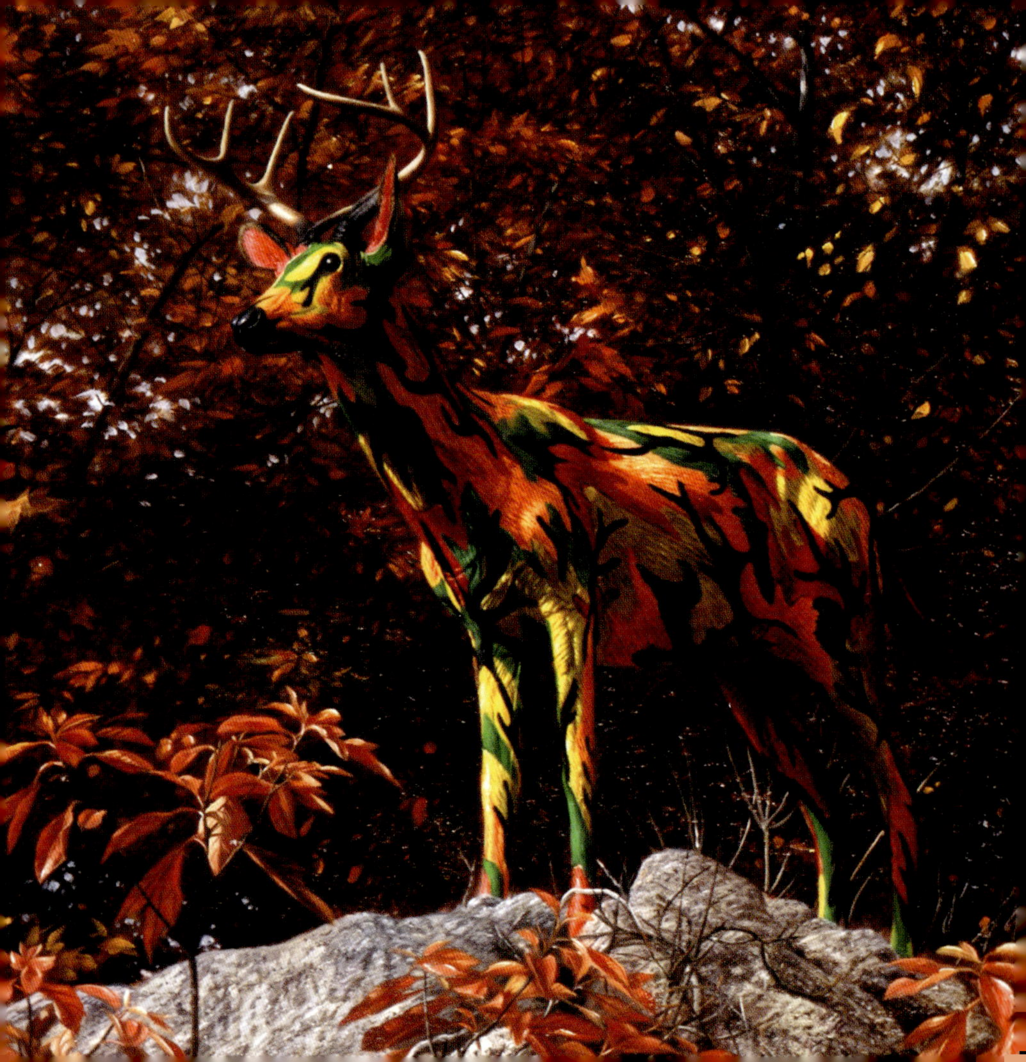

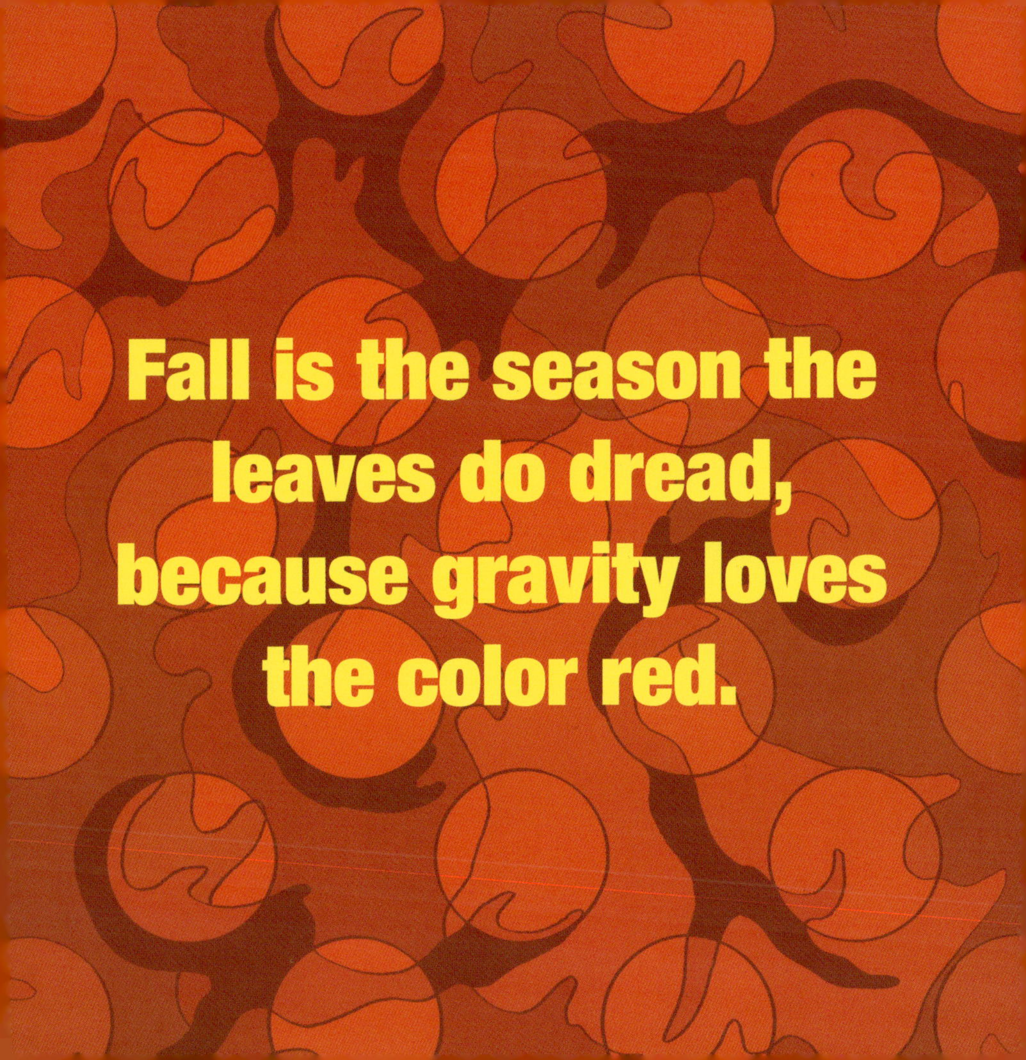
Fall is the season the
leaves do dread,
because gravity loves
the color red.

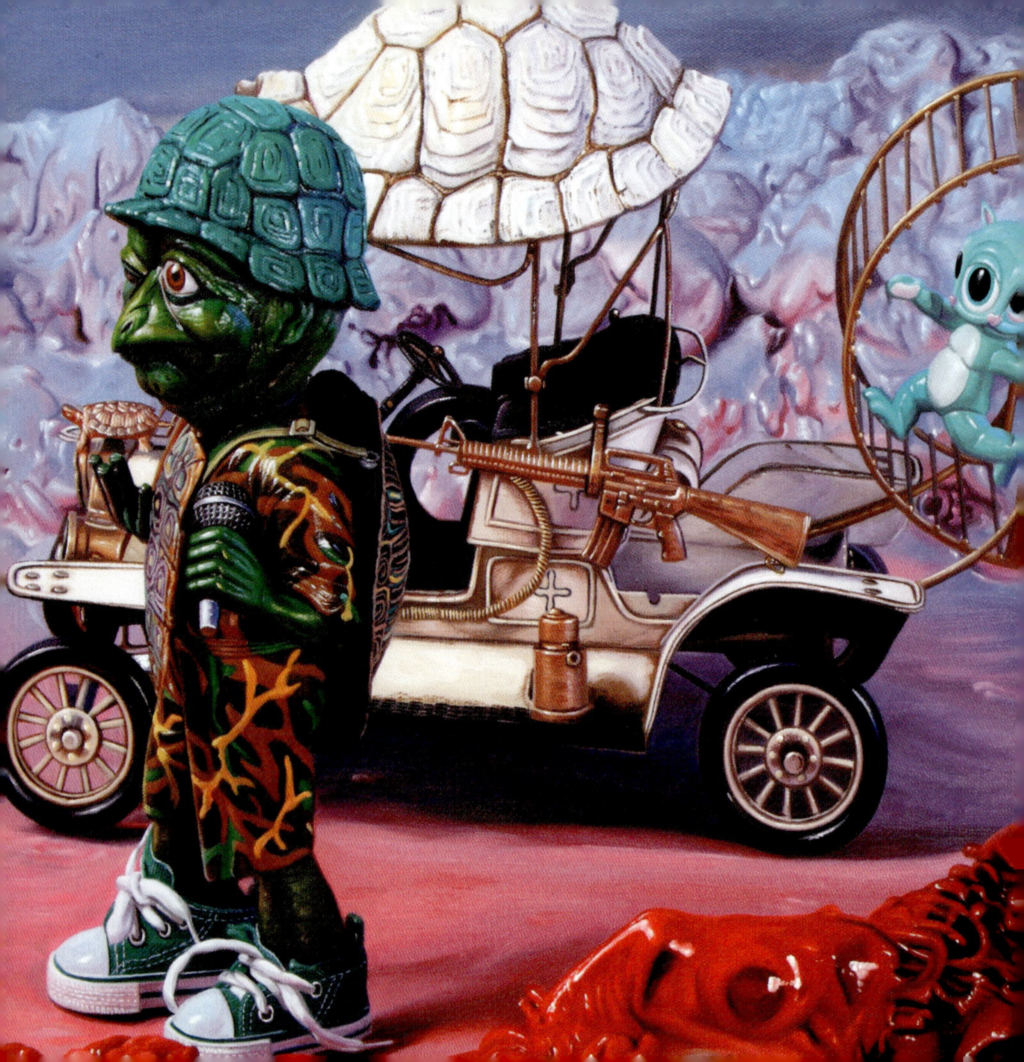

Last place gets to stay in the race longer.

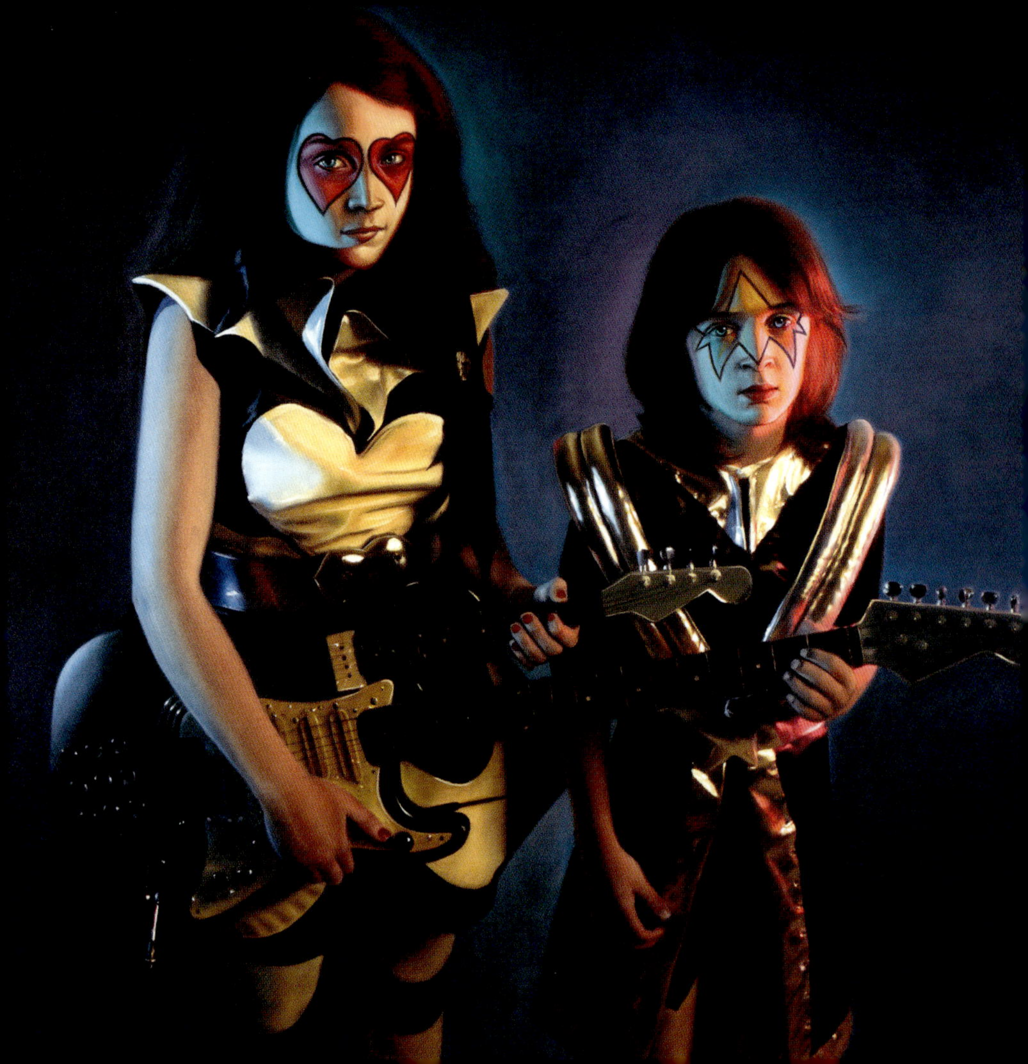

When all else fails, start a band.

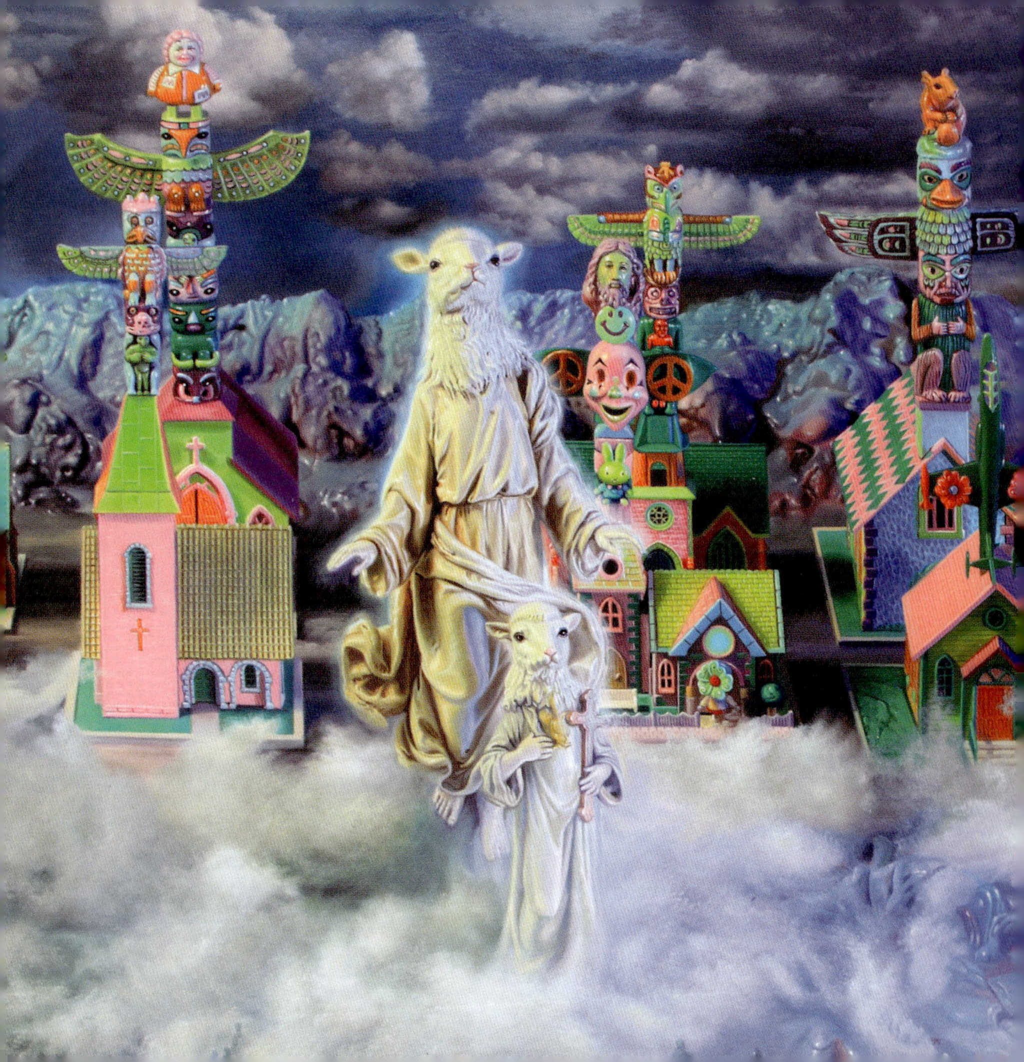

In Heaven, no one can hear you dream.

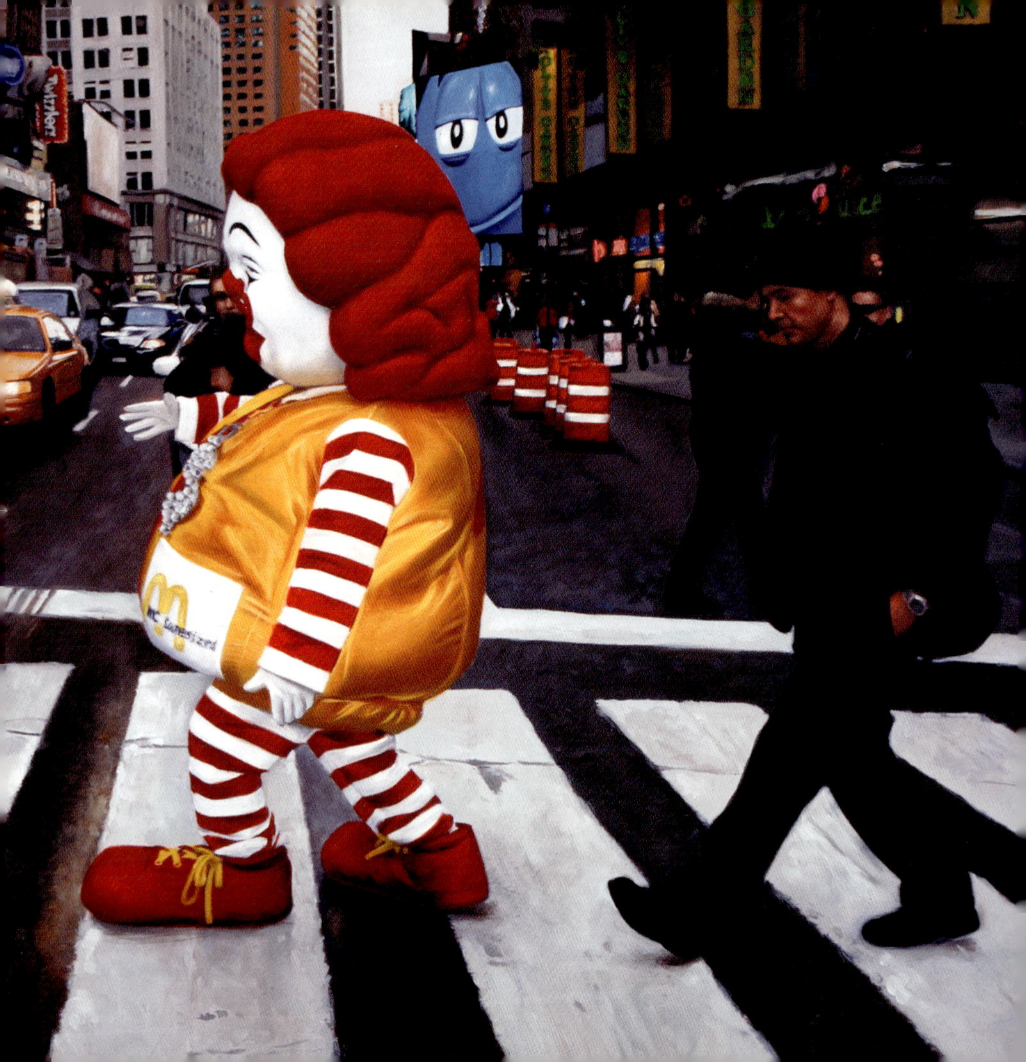
Twizzlers
Mc Supersized

Behind every great man is a pickpocket.

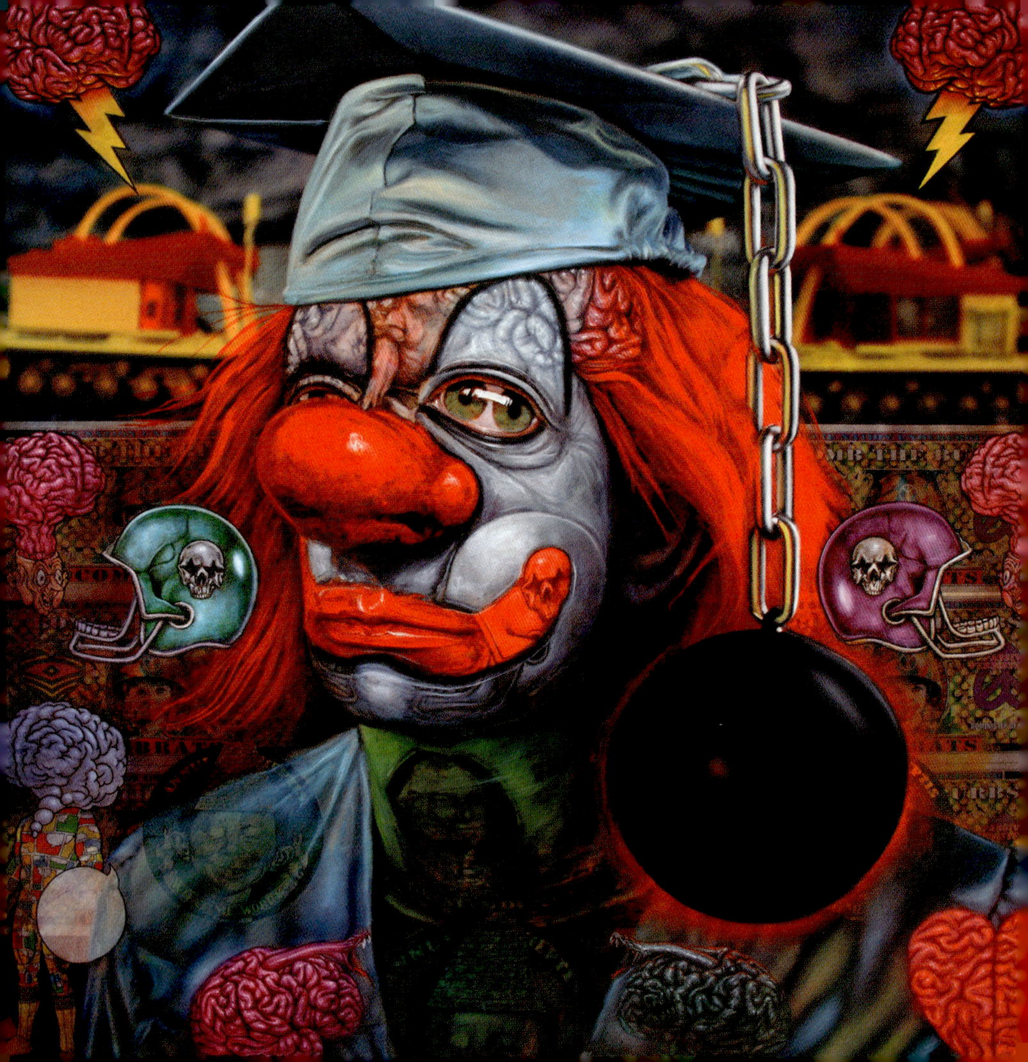

Education prepares the next generation for life and debt.

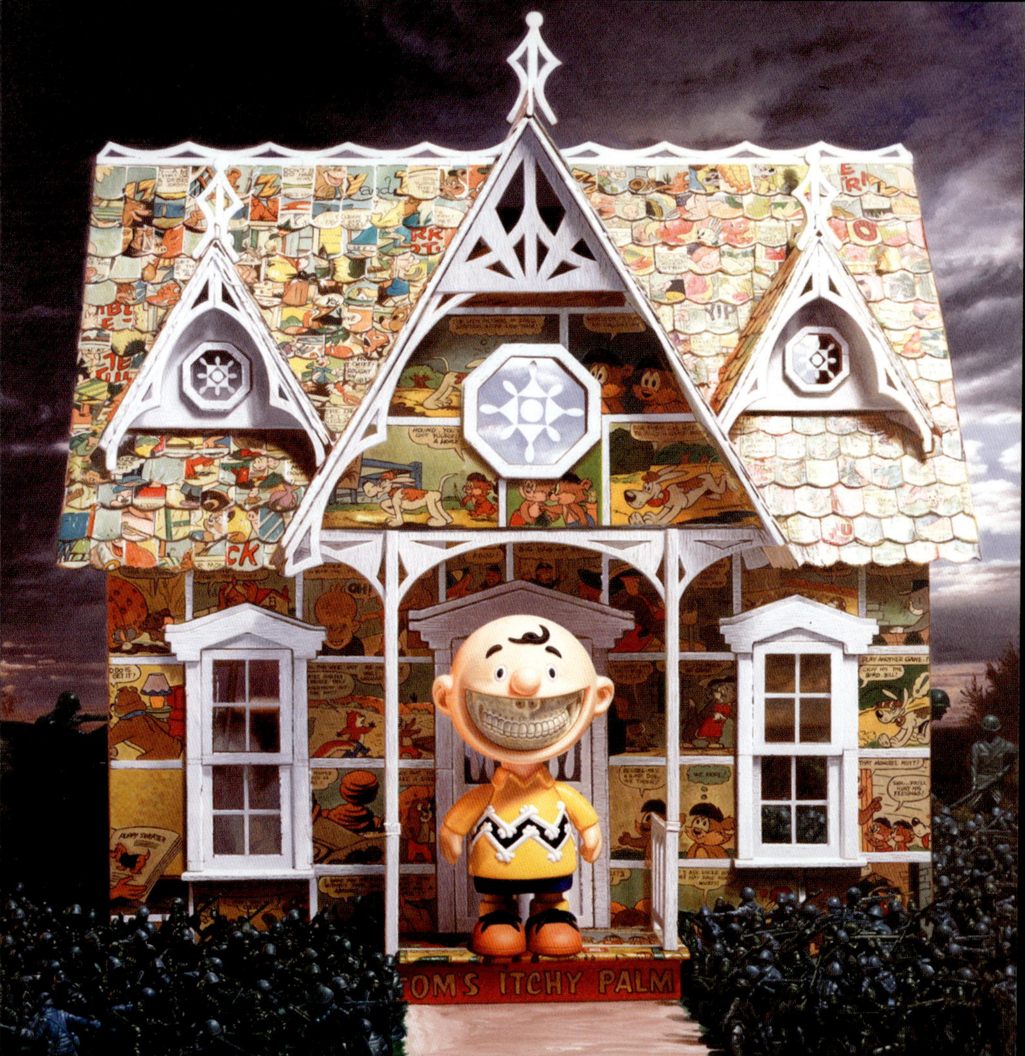
OM'S ITCHY PALM

I pray my obituary is a hoax.

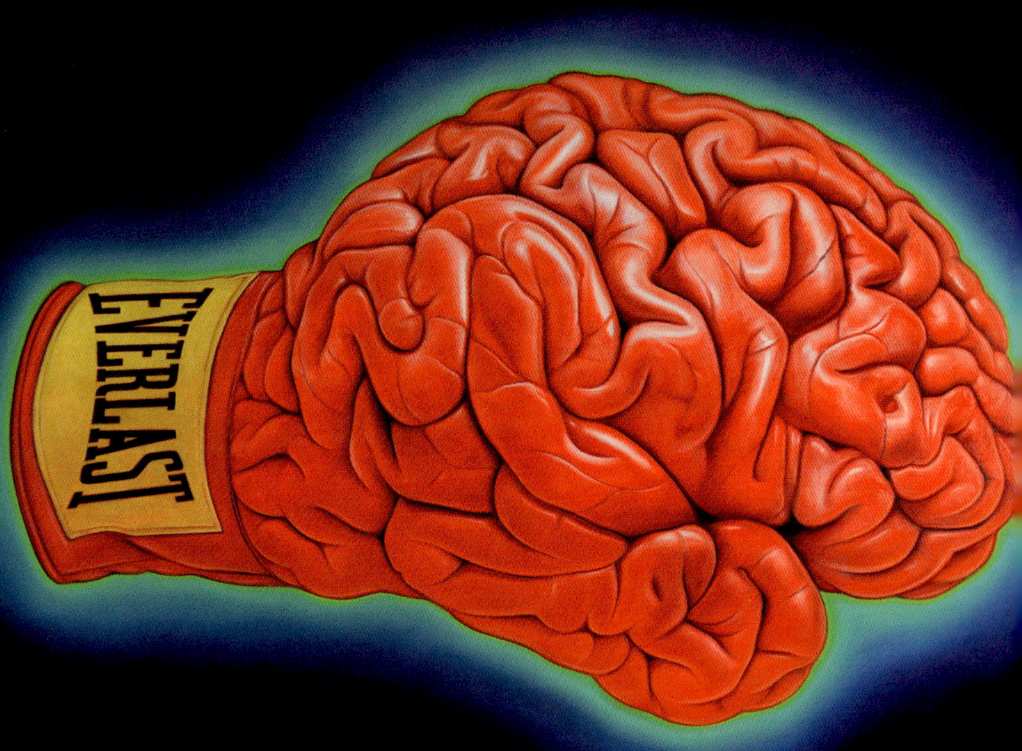
EVERLAST

No brain, no pain.

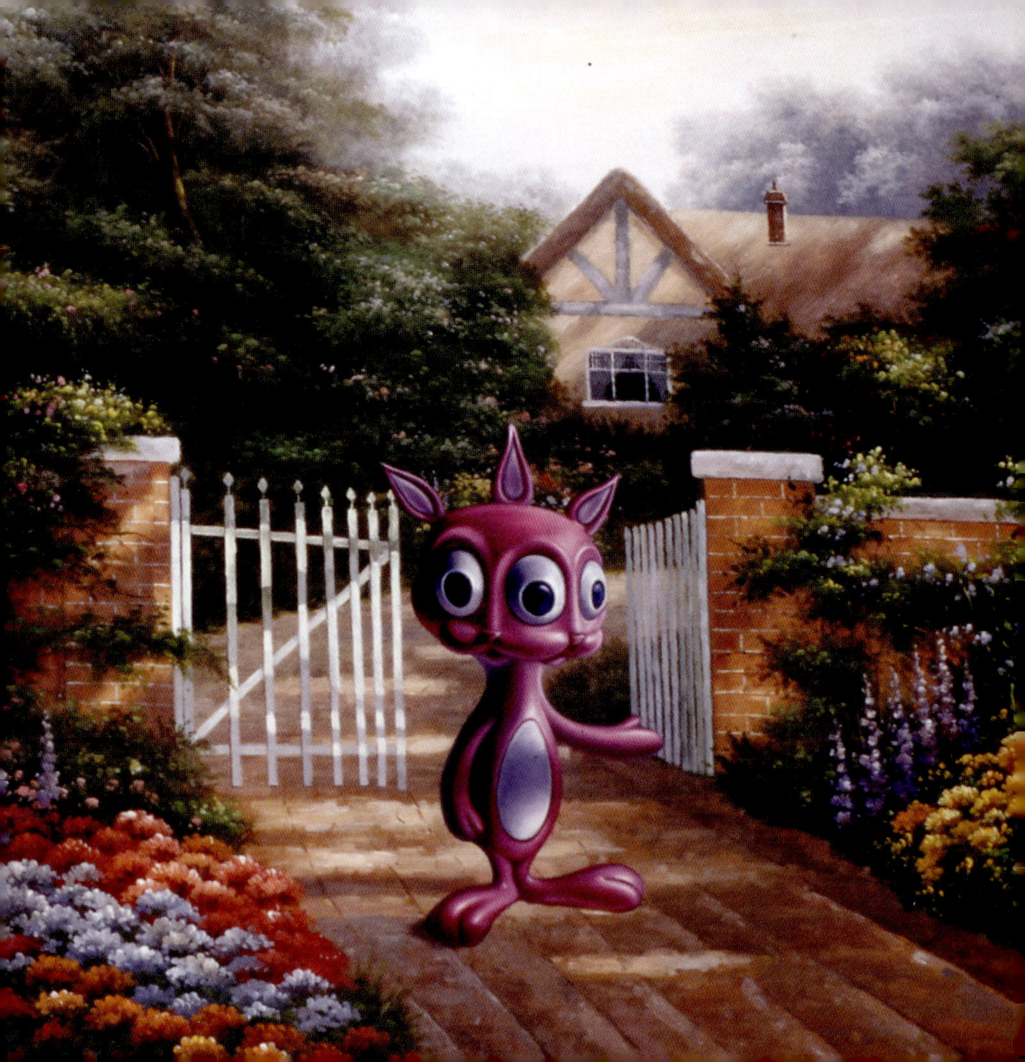

You can't have your kitsch and your good taste too.

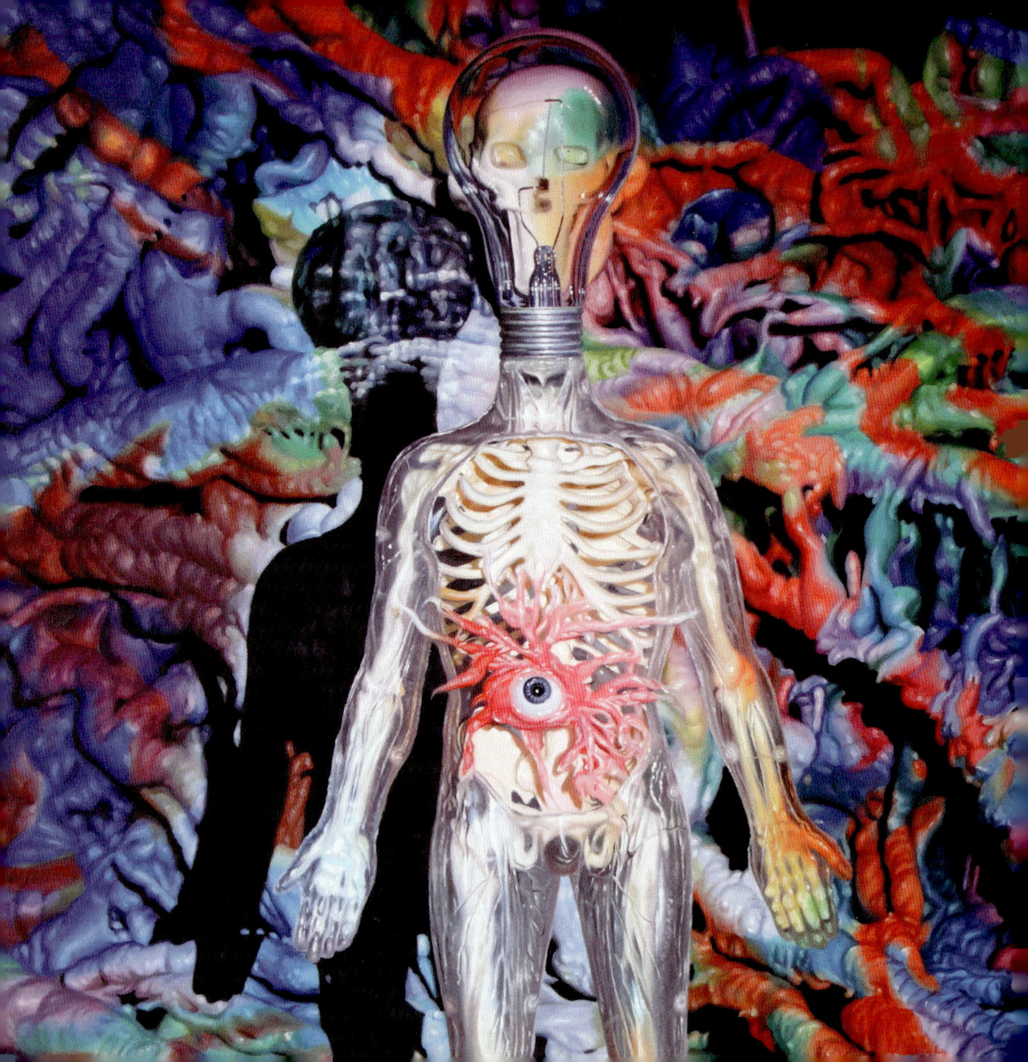

Madness is the genius' substitute for stupidity.

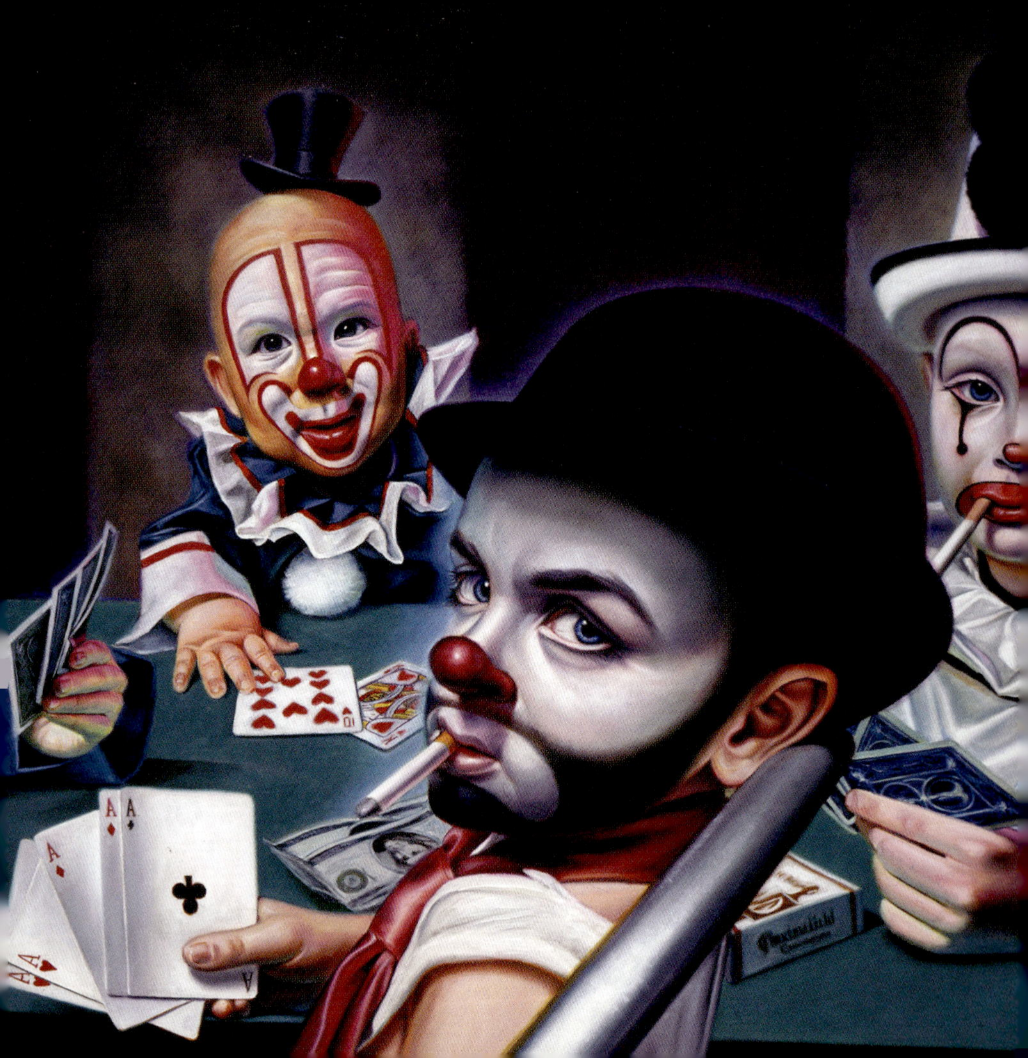

Nothing is true until someone believes.

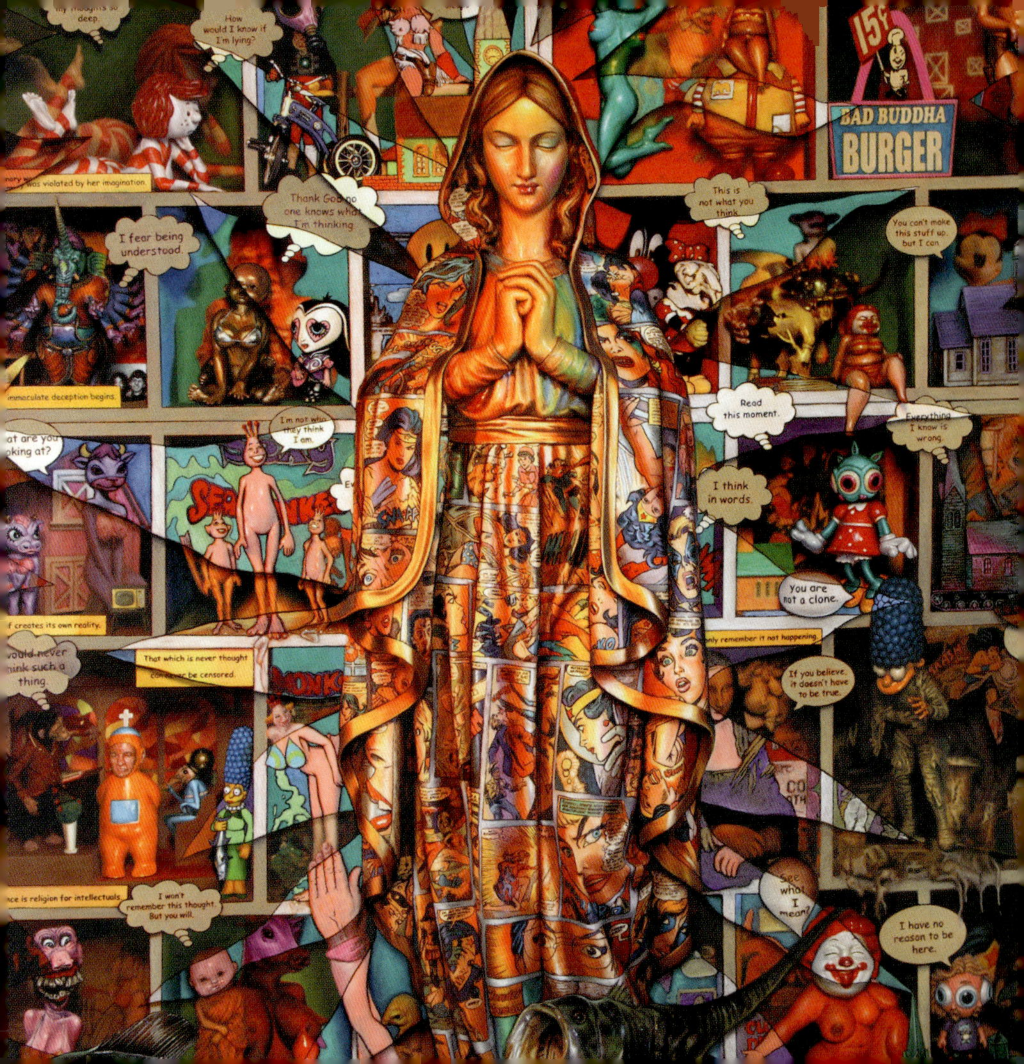
deep.
How would I know if I'm lying?
was violated by her imagination.
15¢
BAD BUDDHA
BURGER
I fear being understood.
Thank God no one knows what I'm thinking.
This is not what you think.
You can't make this stuff up, but I can.
mmaculate deception begins.
I'm not who they think I am.
Read this moment.
Everything I know is wrong.
I think in words.
You are not a clone.
creates its own reality.
That which is never thought can never be censored.
only remember it not happening.
If you believe, it doesn't have to be true.
thing.
nce is religion for intellectuals.
I won't remember this thought. But you will.
See what I mean?
I have no reason to be here.

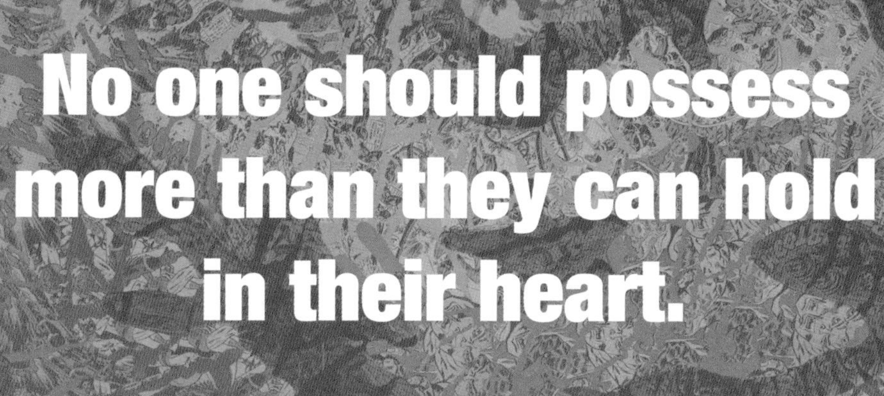
No one should possess
more than they can hold
in their heart.

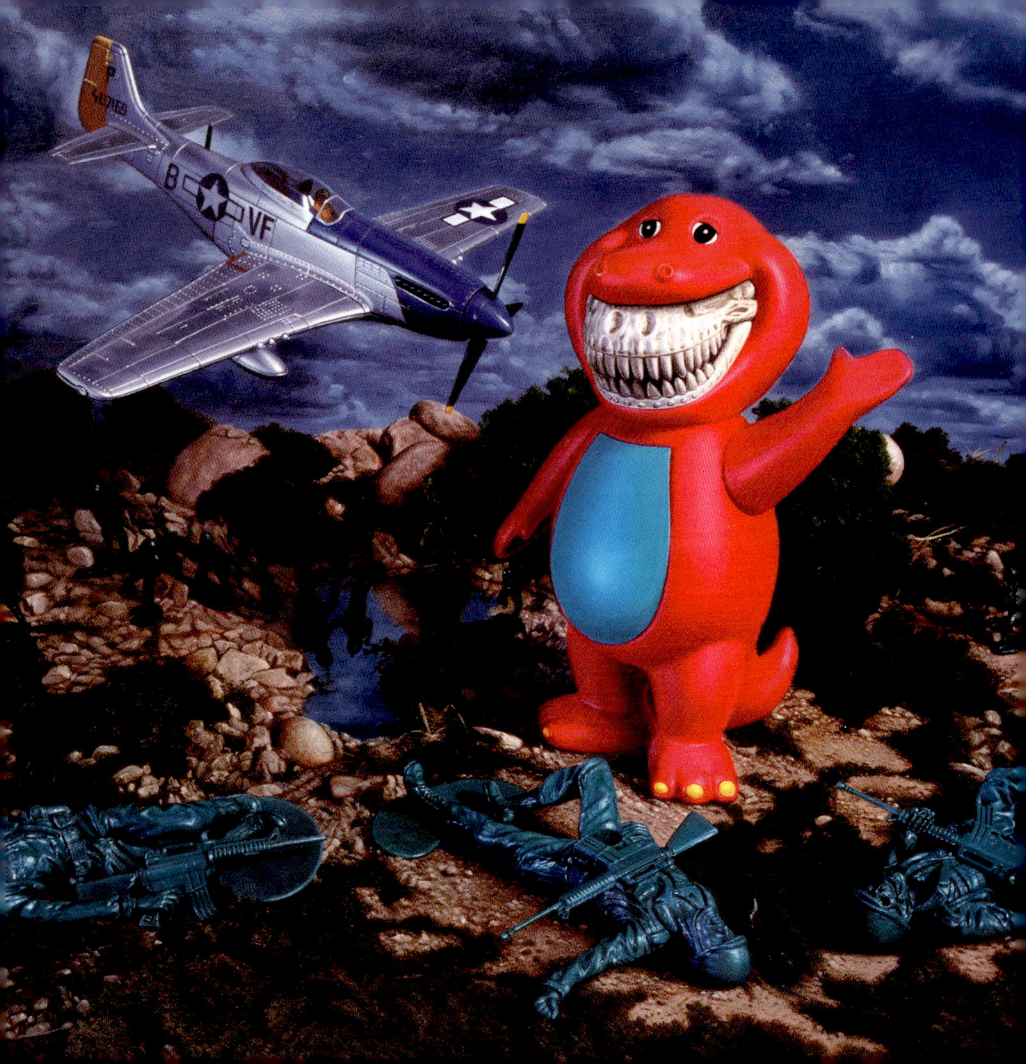
B
VF

If questioning something endangers its existence, extinction is probably in its future.

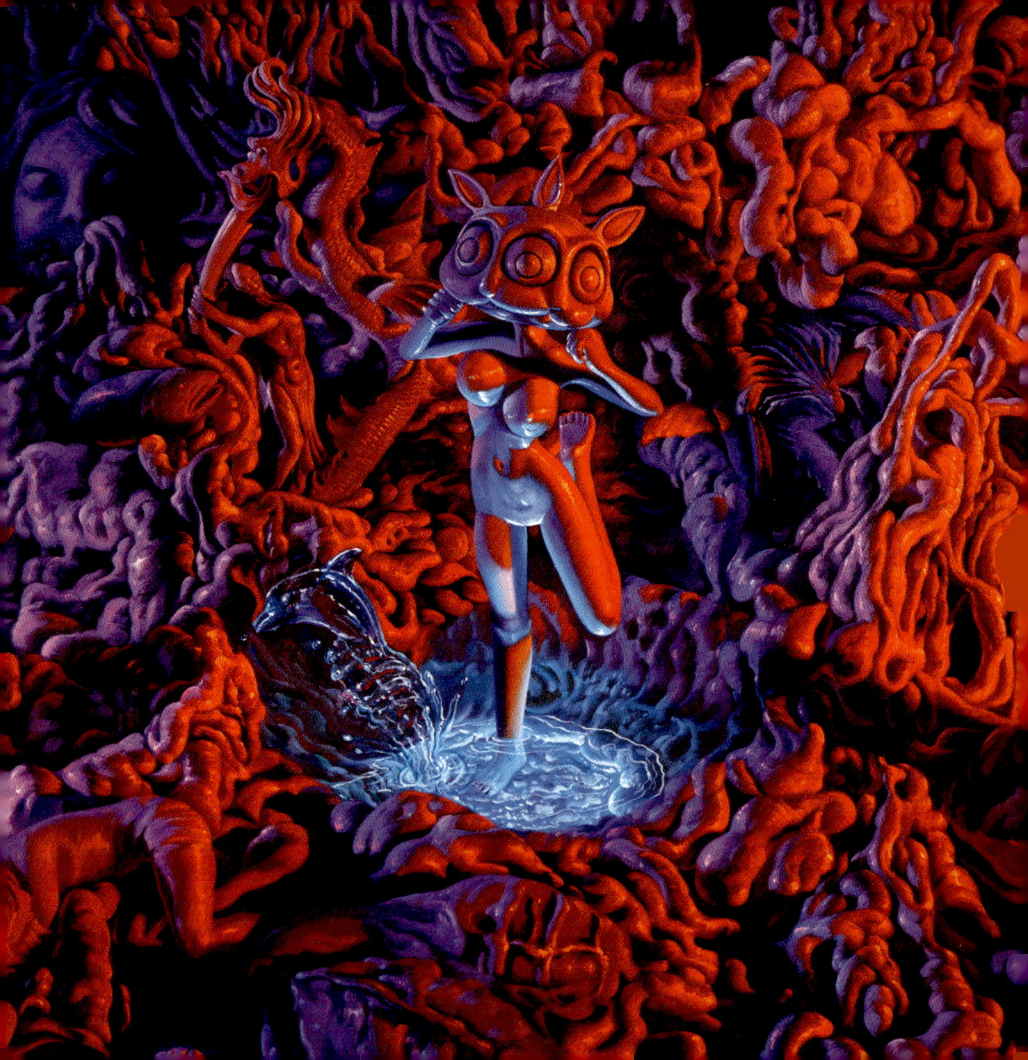

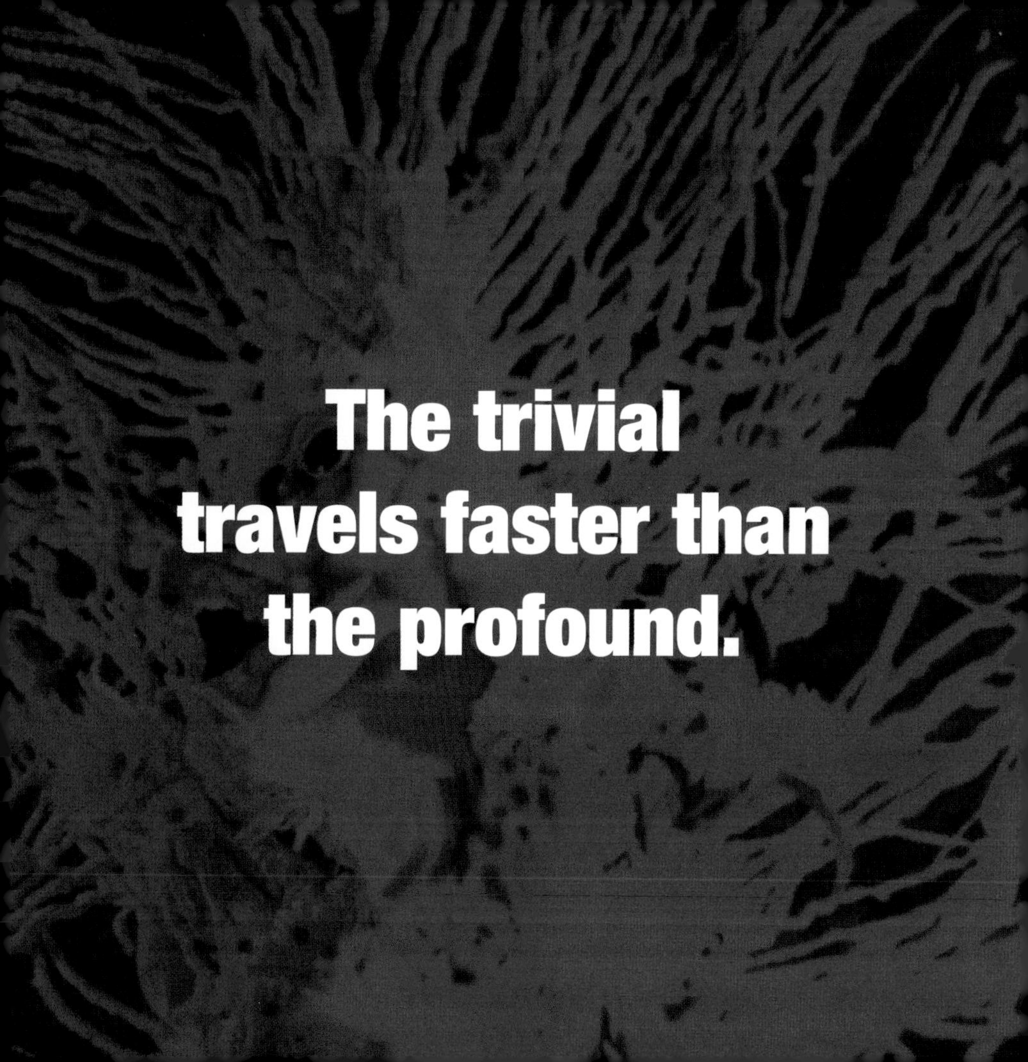
The trivial
travels faster than
the profound.

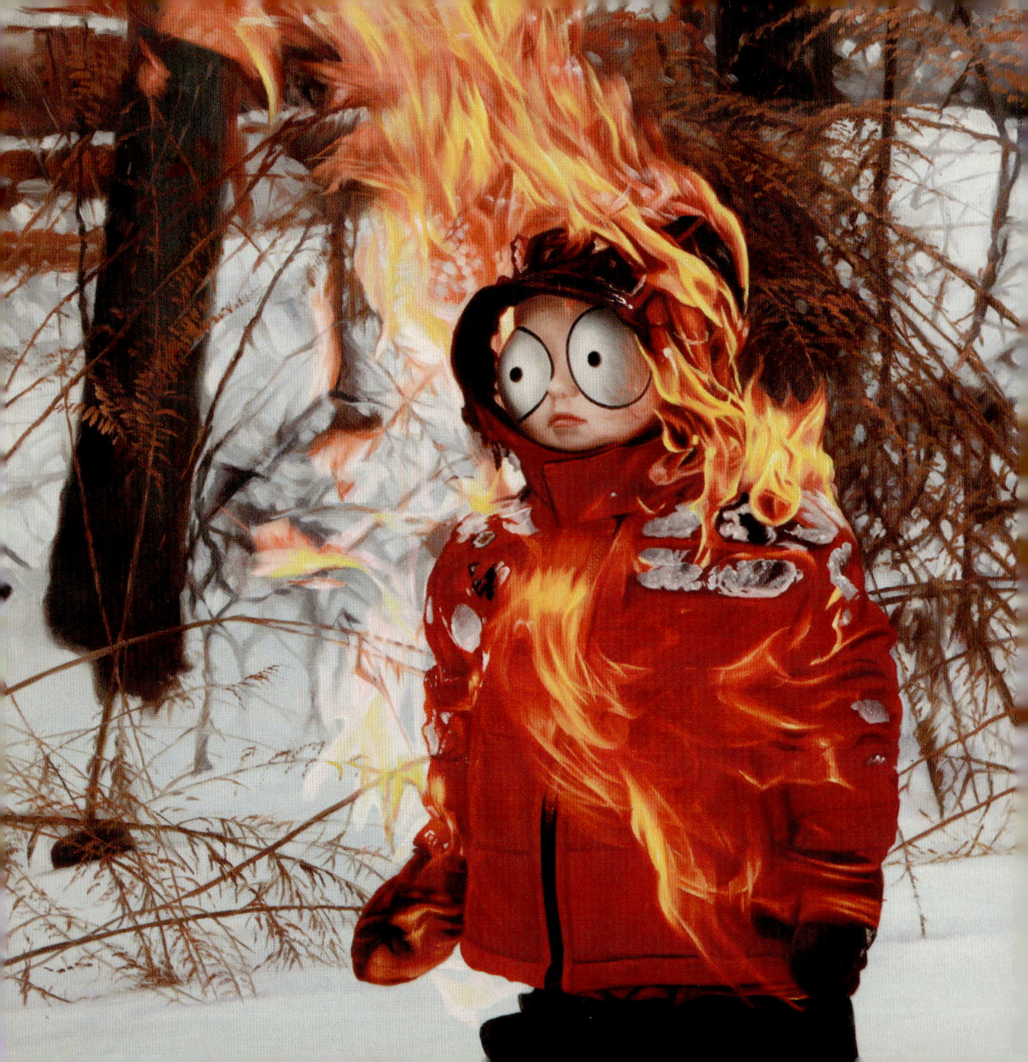

Some days you can't see the forest for the fire.

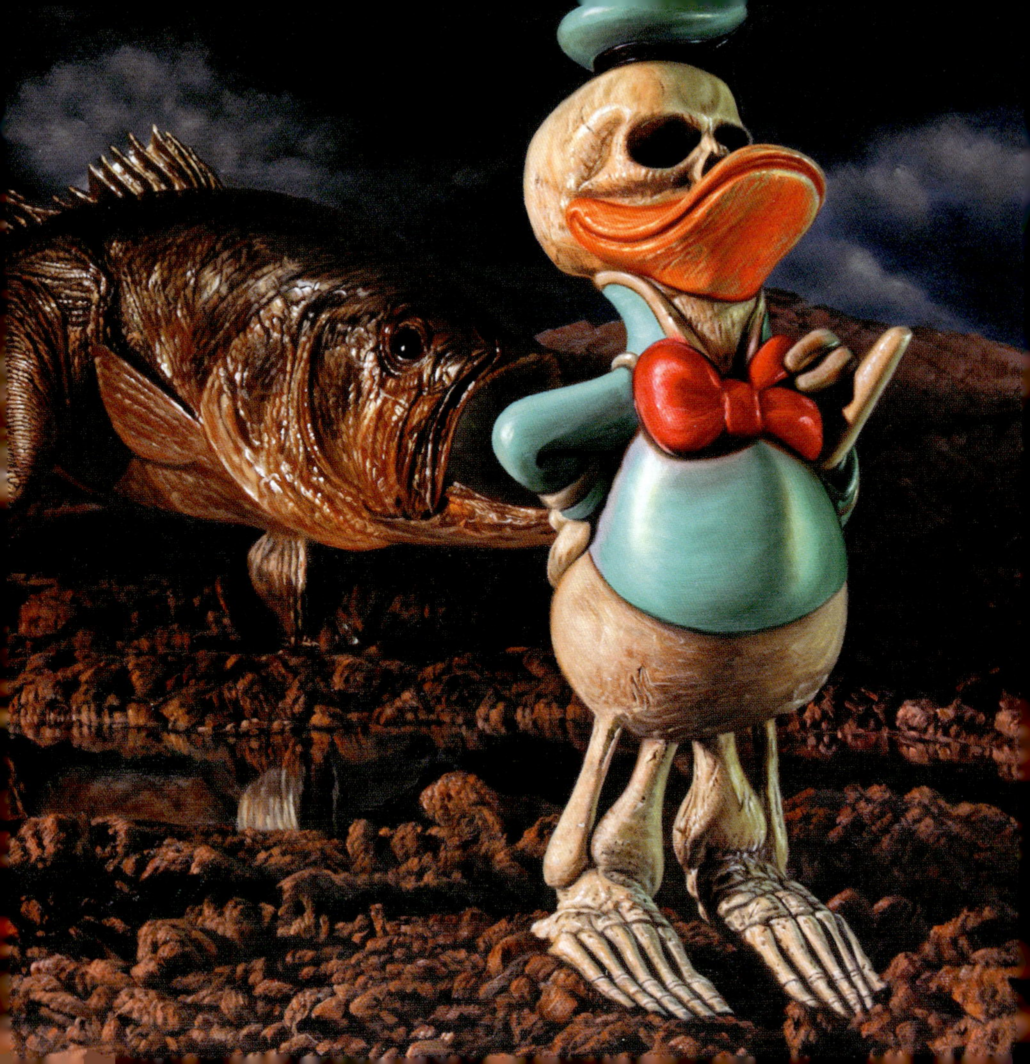

You're guaranteed a past, but not a future.

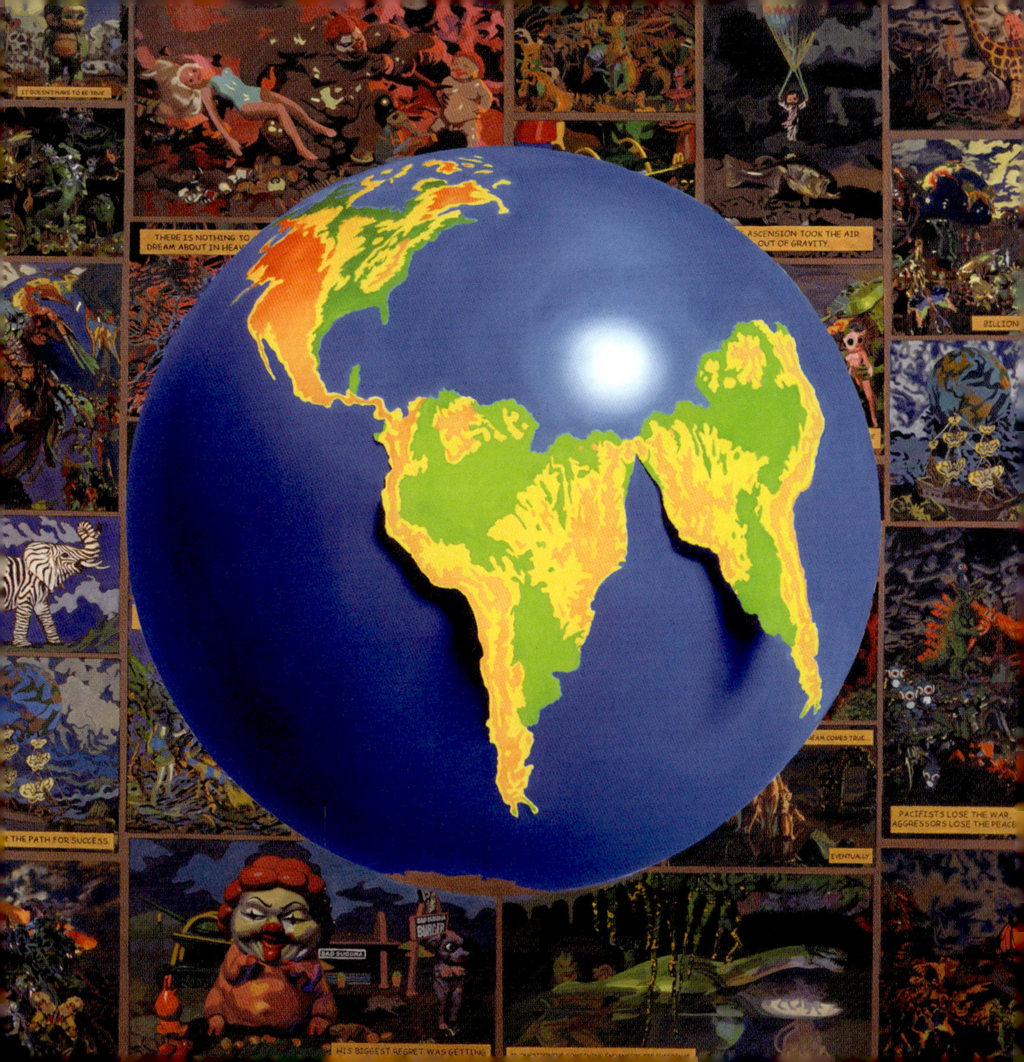
IT DOESN'T HAVE TO BE TRUE
THERE IS NOTHING TO
ASCENSION TOOK THE AIR
OUT OF GRAVITY
BILLION
PACIFISTS LOSE THE WAR,
AGGRESSORS LOSE THE PEACE
EVENTUALLY
THE PATH FOR SUCCESS.
BAD BUDDHA
BURGER
HIS BIGGEST REGRET WAS GETTING

It’s always tomorrow on the other side of the world.

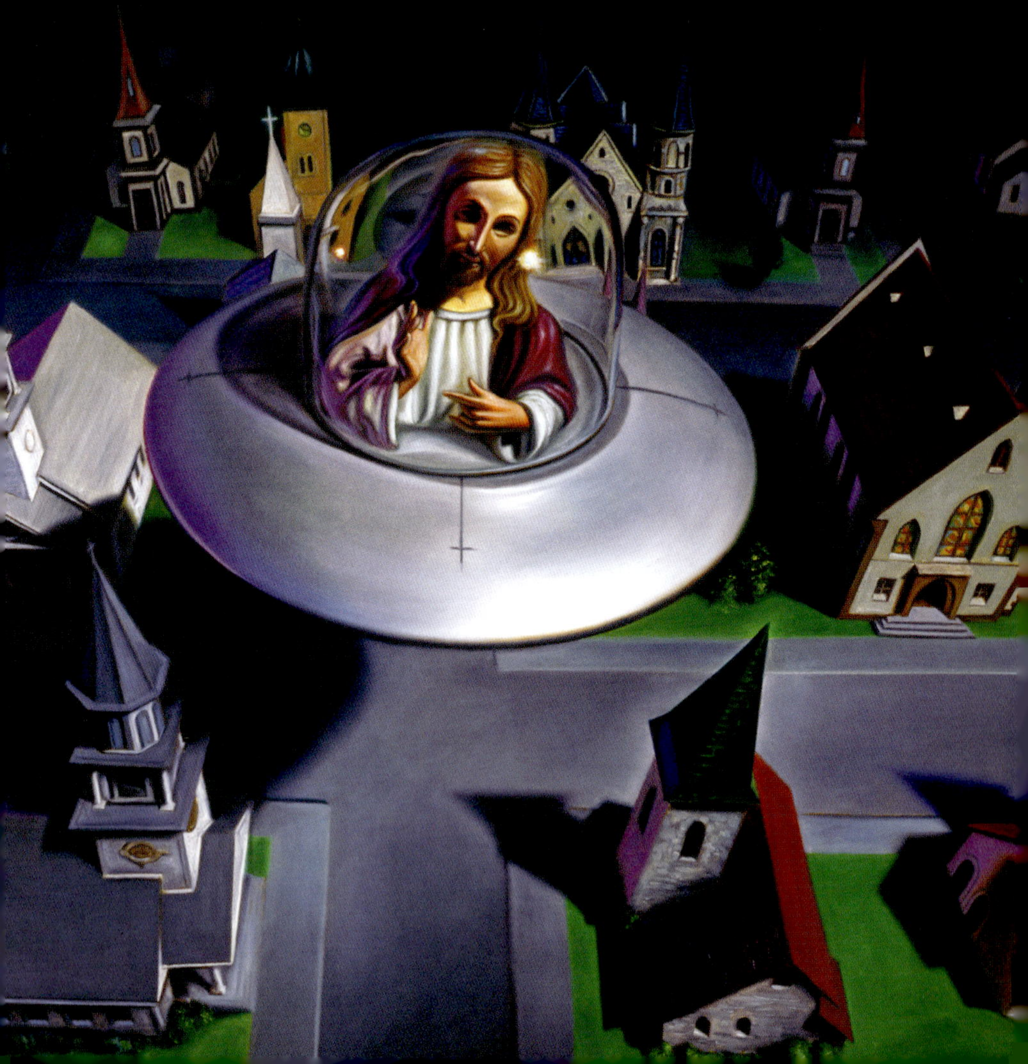

I believe my own imagination.

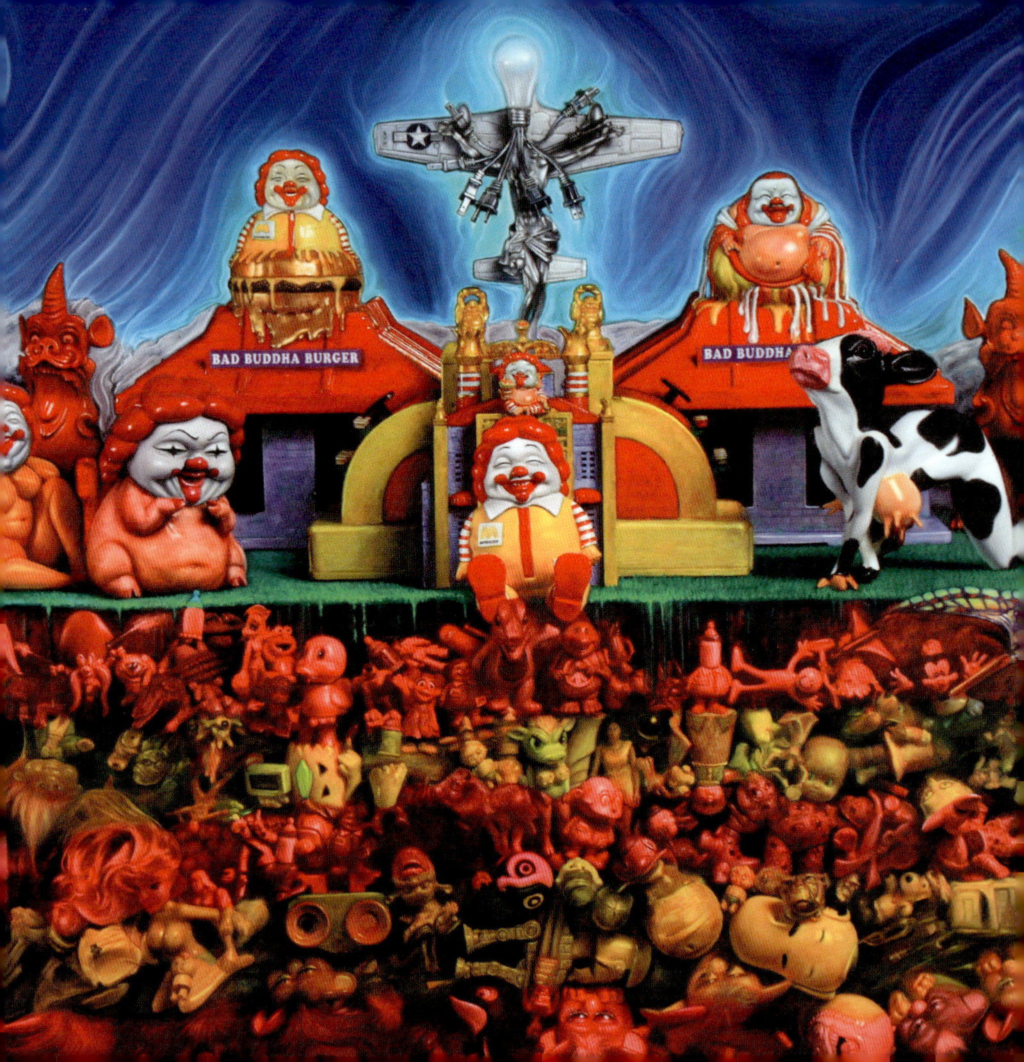
BAD BUDDHA BURGER
BAD BUDDHA

Memories forever
remake themselves.

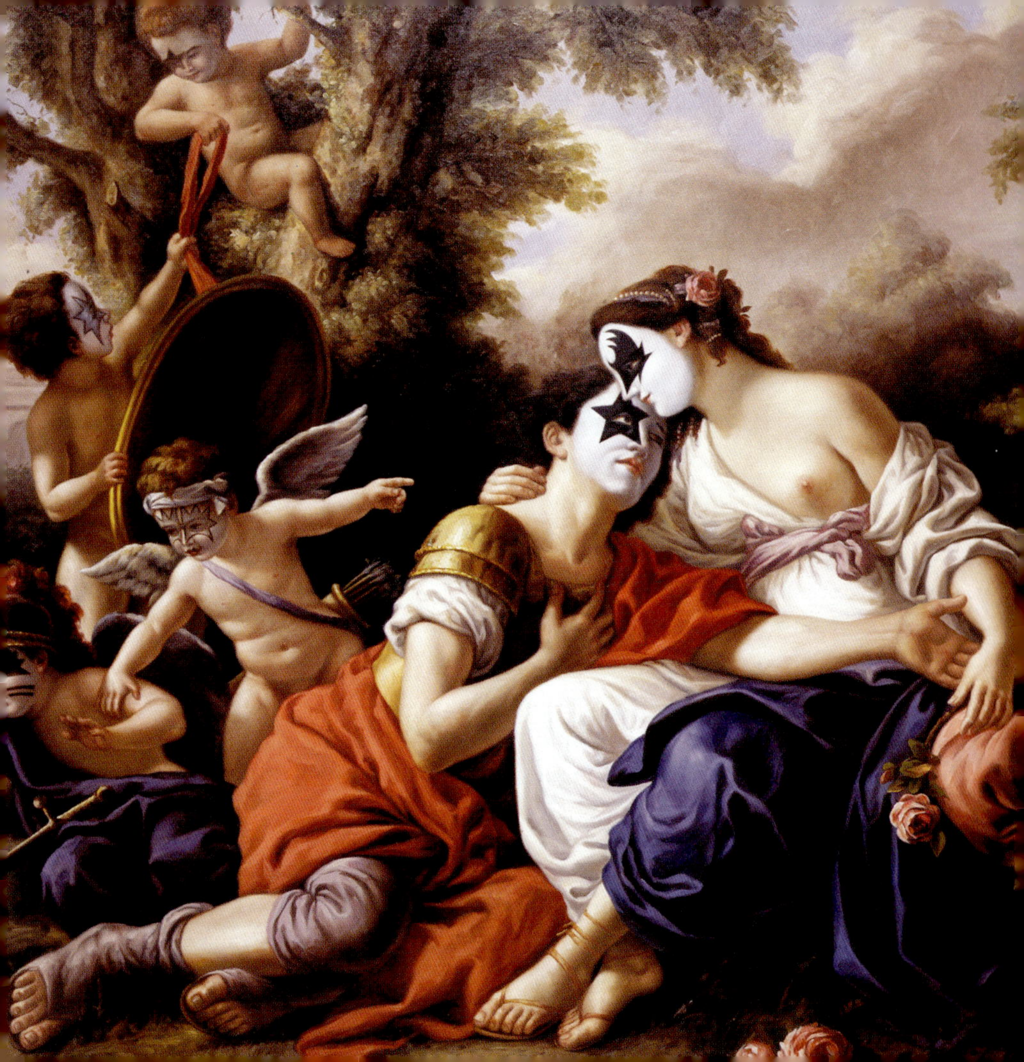

Myths are the unbelievable truth.

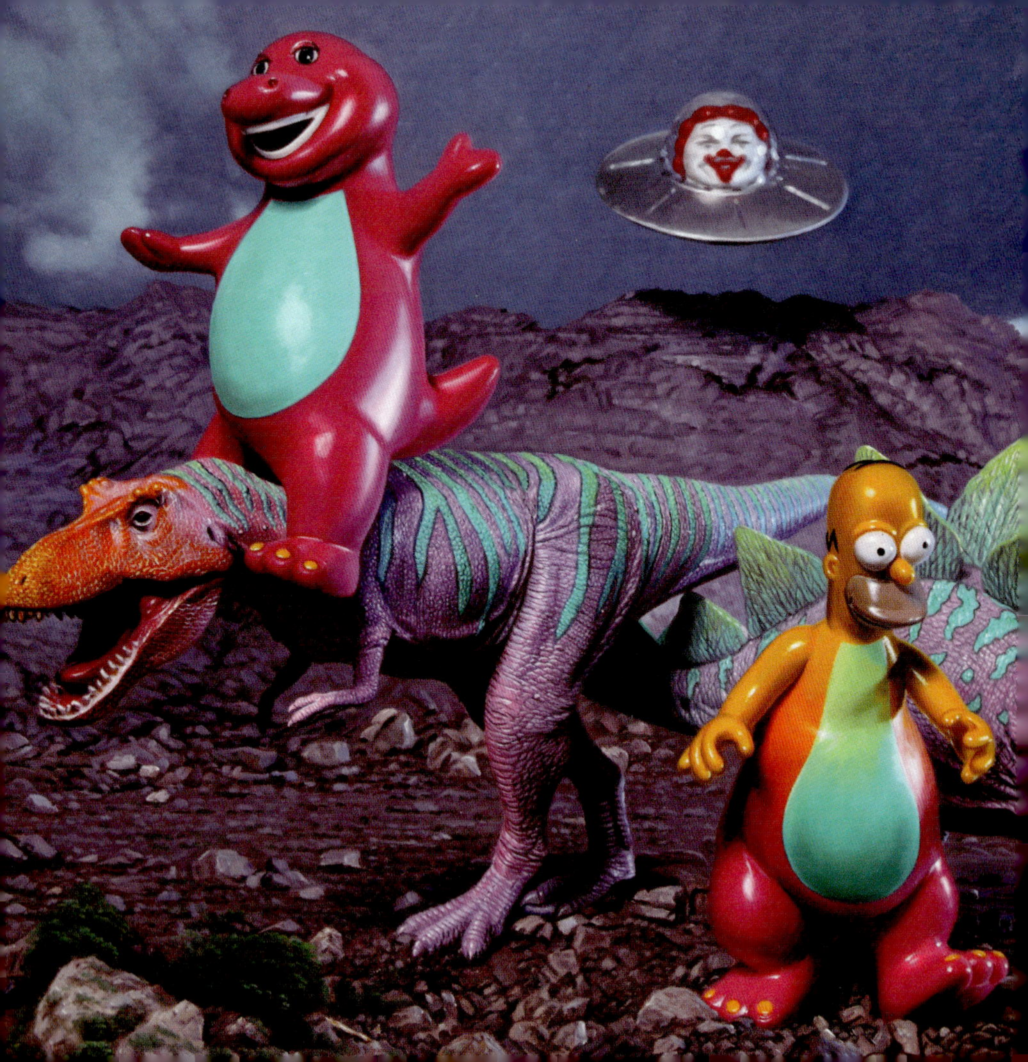

Evolution is a two-way street.

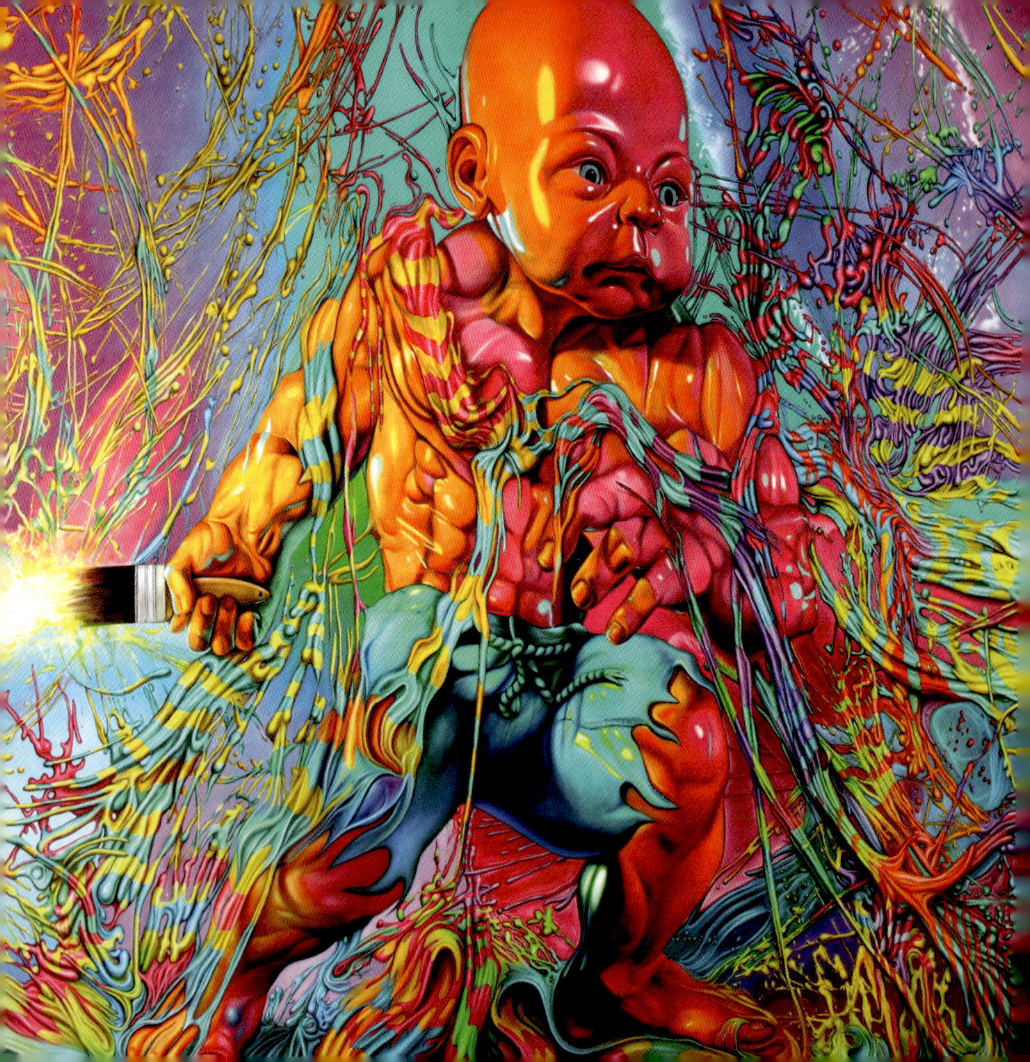

It's not the size of the brush; it's the expanse of the imagination.

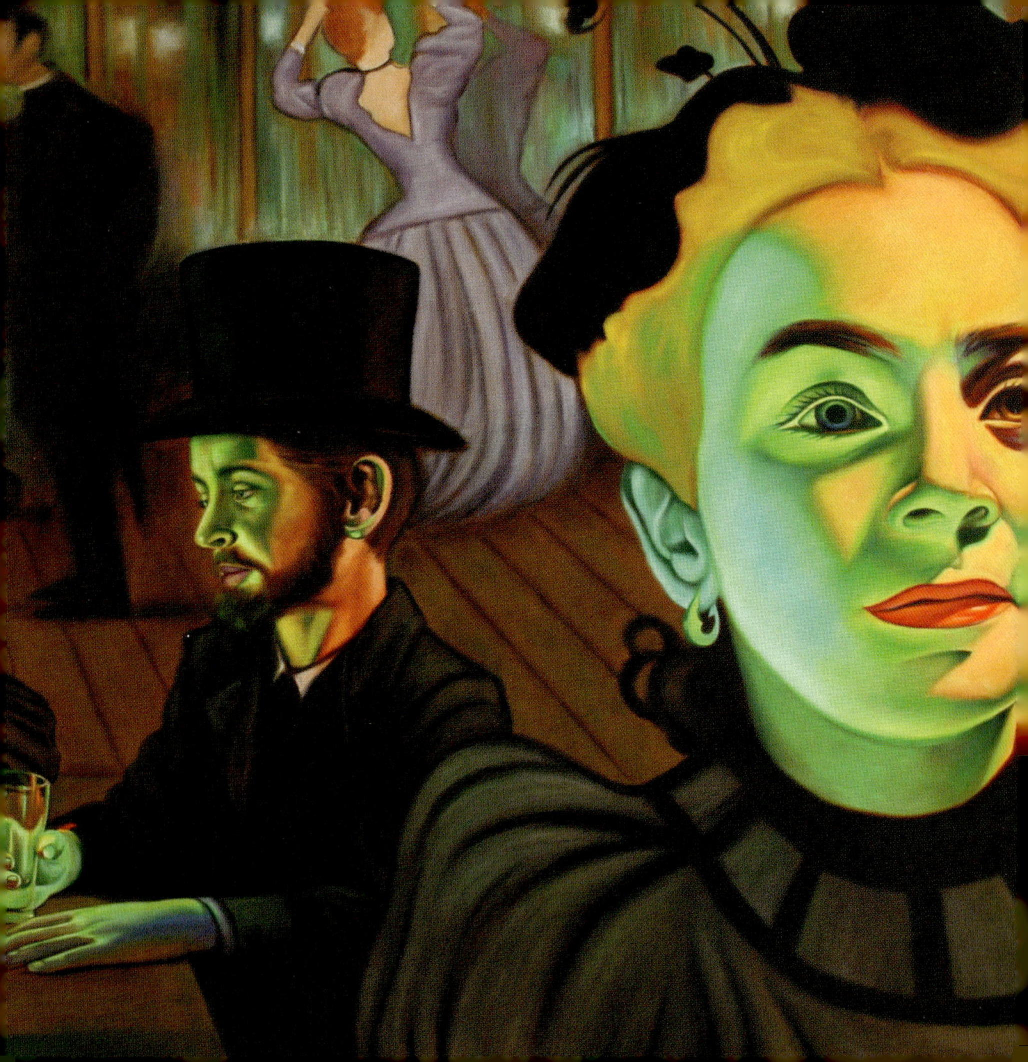

Absinthe makes the mind go wander.

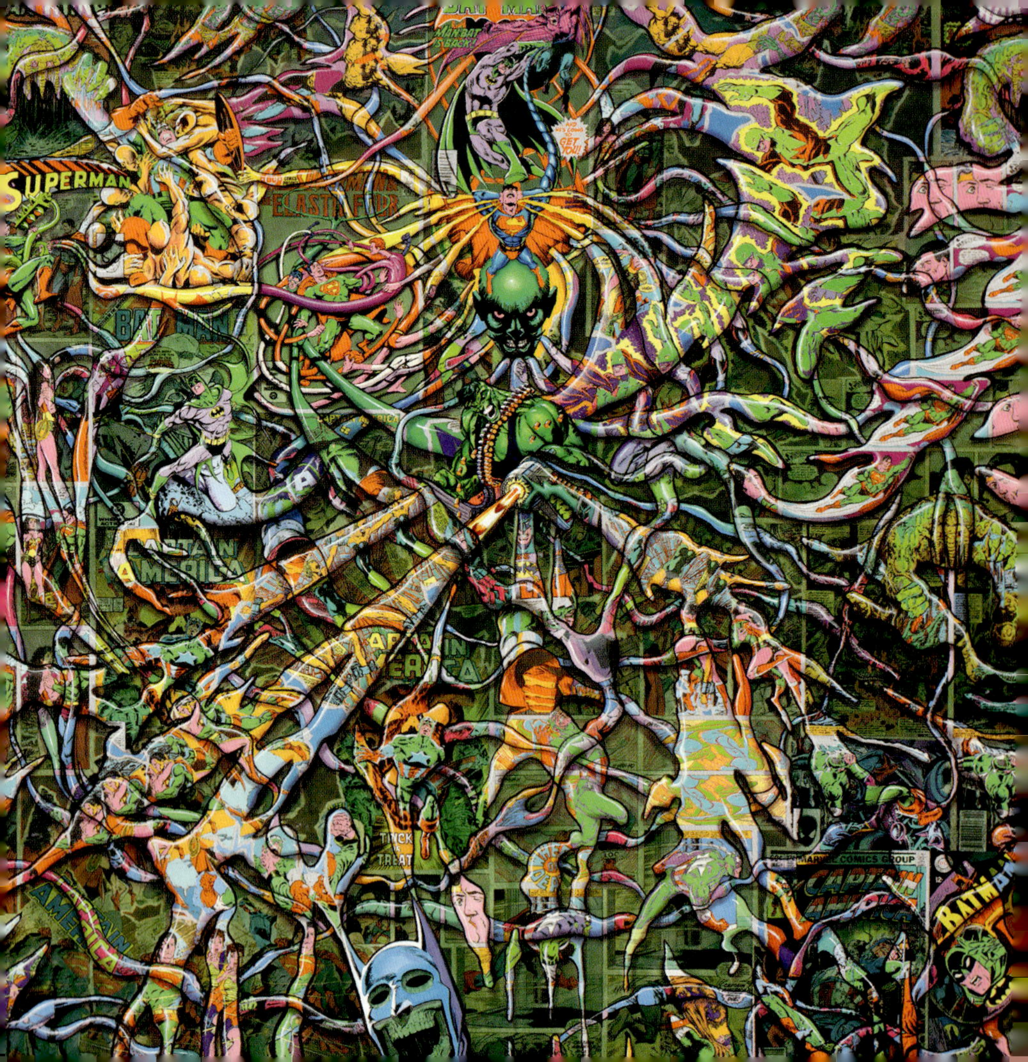

SUPERMAN
MAN-BAT IS BACK!
AND HE'S GOING TO GET YOU!!
BAT MAN
CAPTAIN AMERICA
MARVEL COMICS GROUP

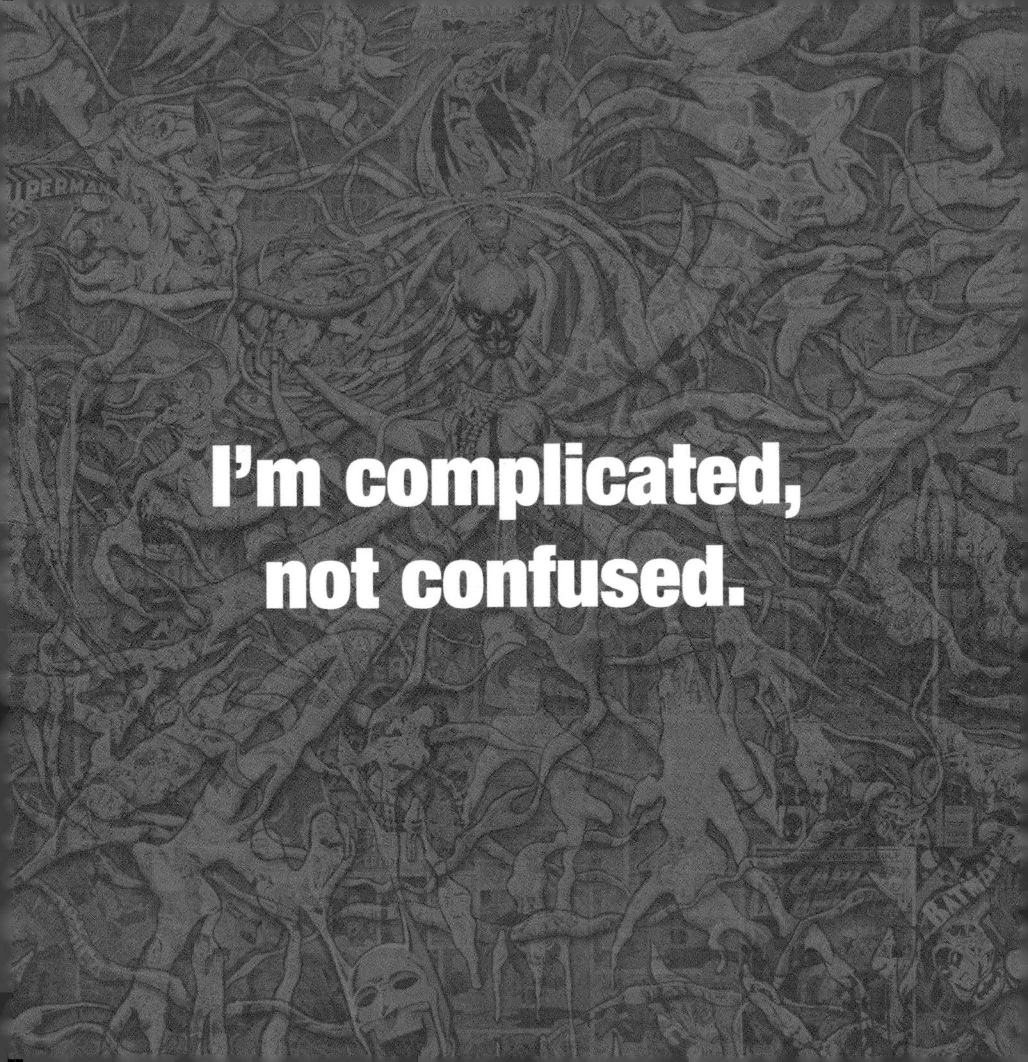
I’m complicated,
not confused.

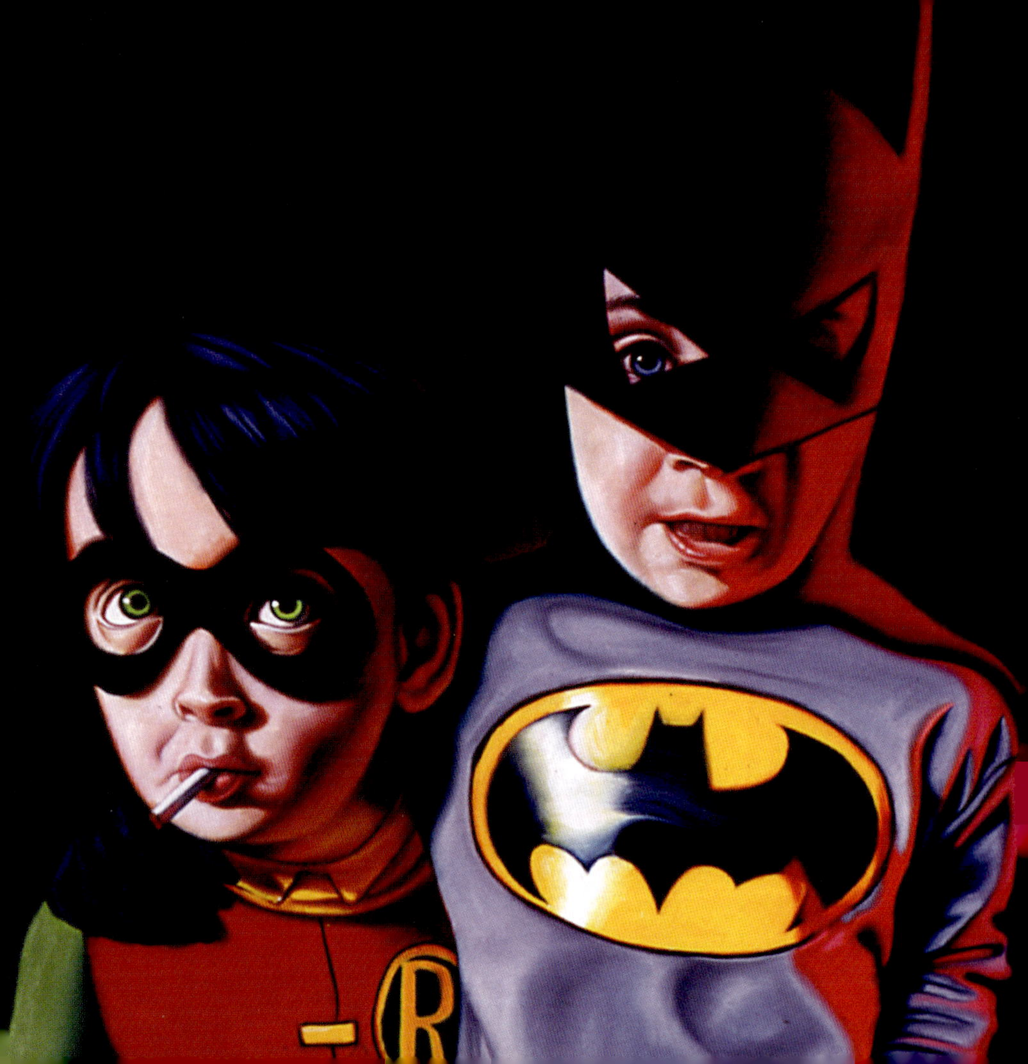

Adversity is the mother of contention.

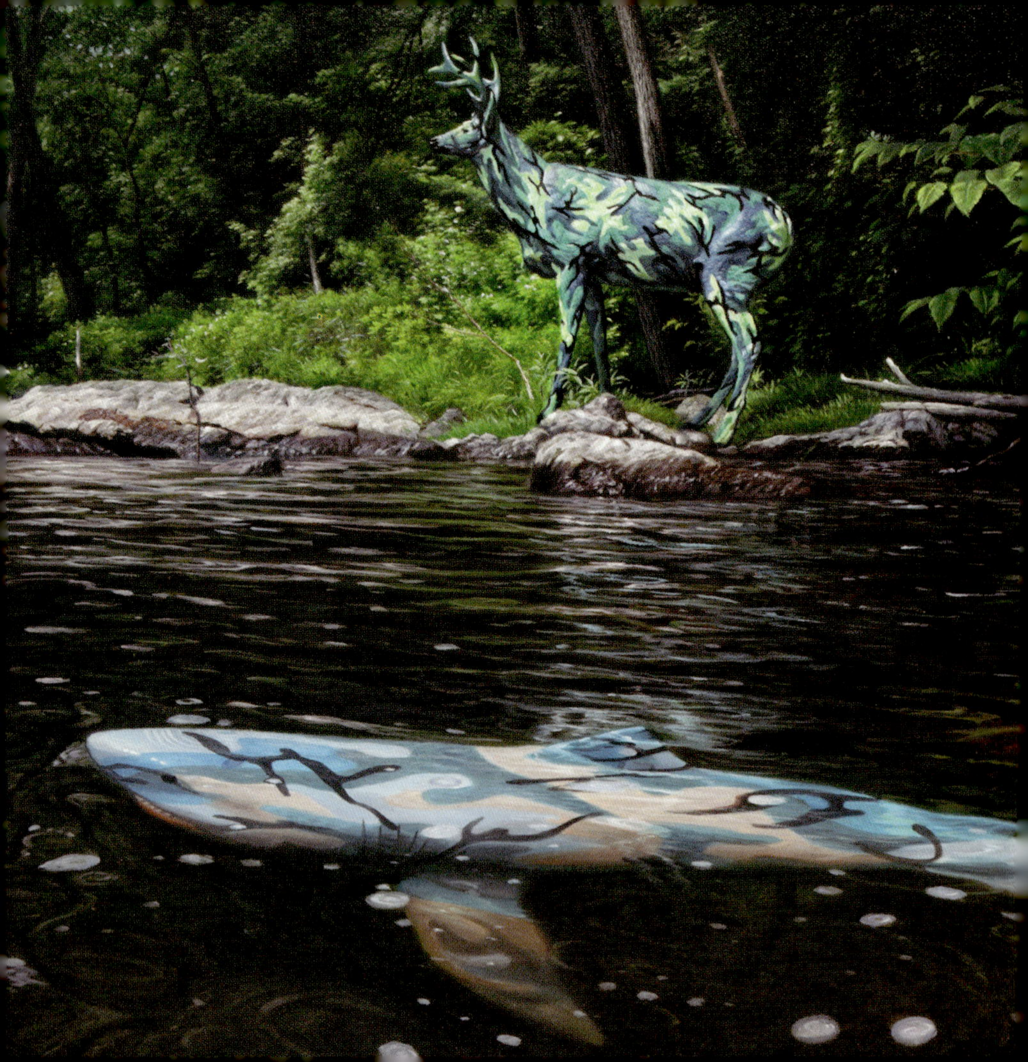

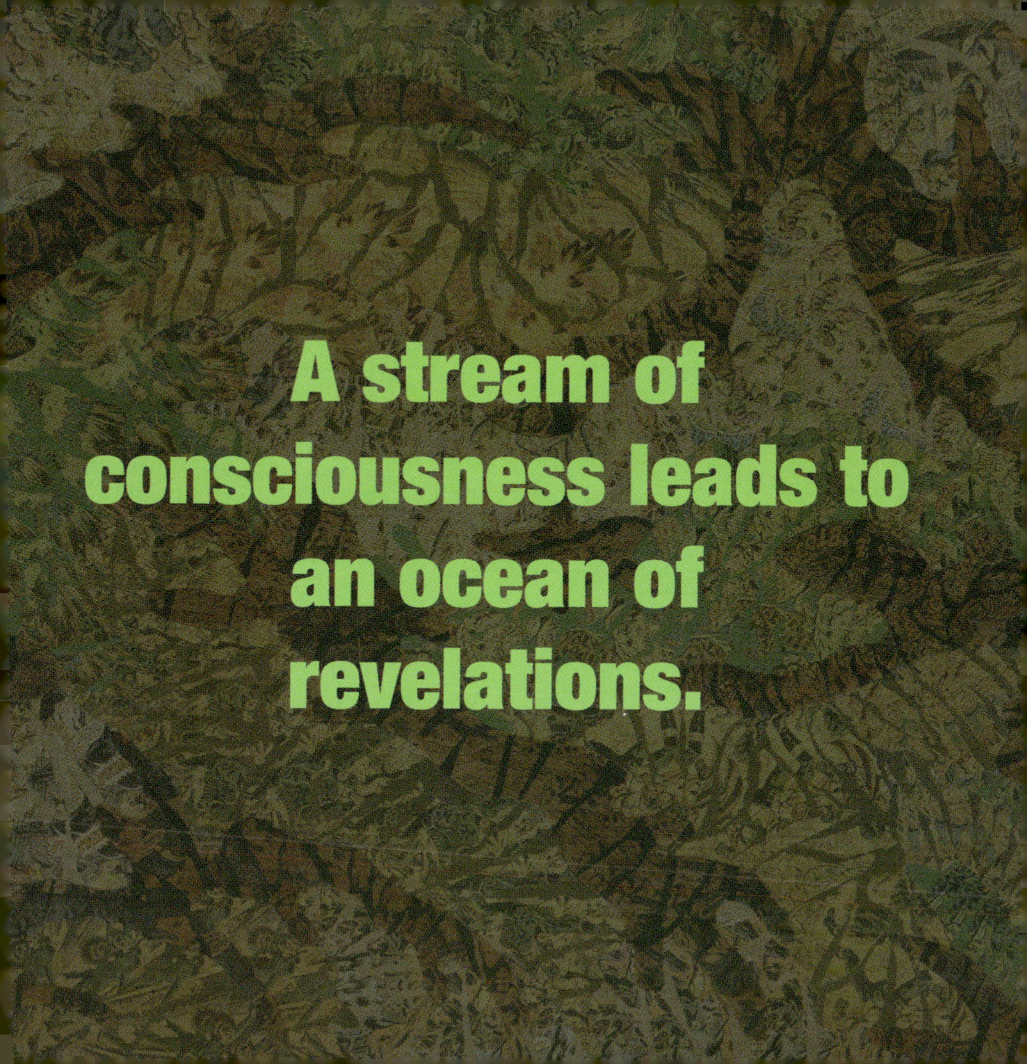
A stream of
consciousness leads to
an ocean of
revelations.

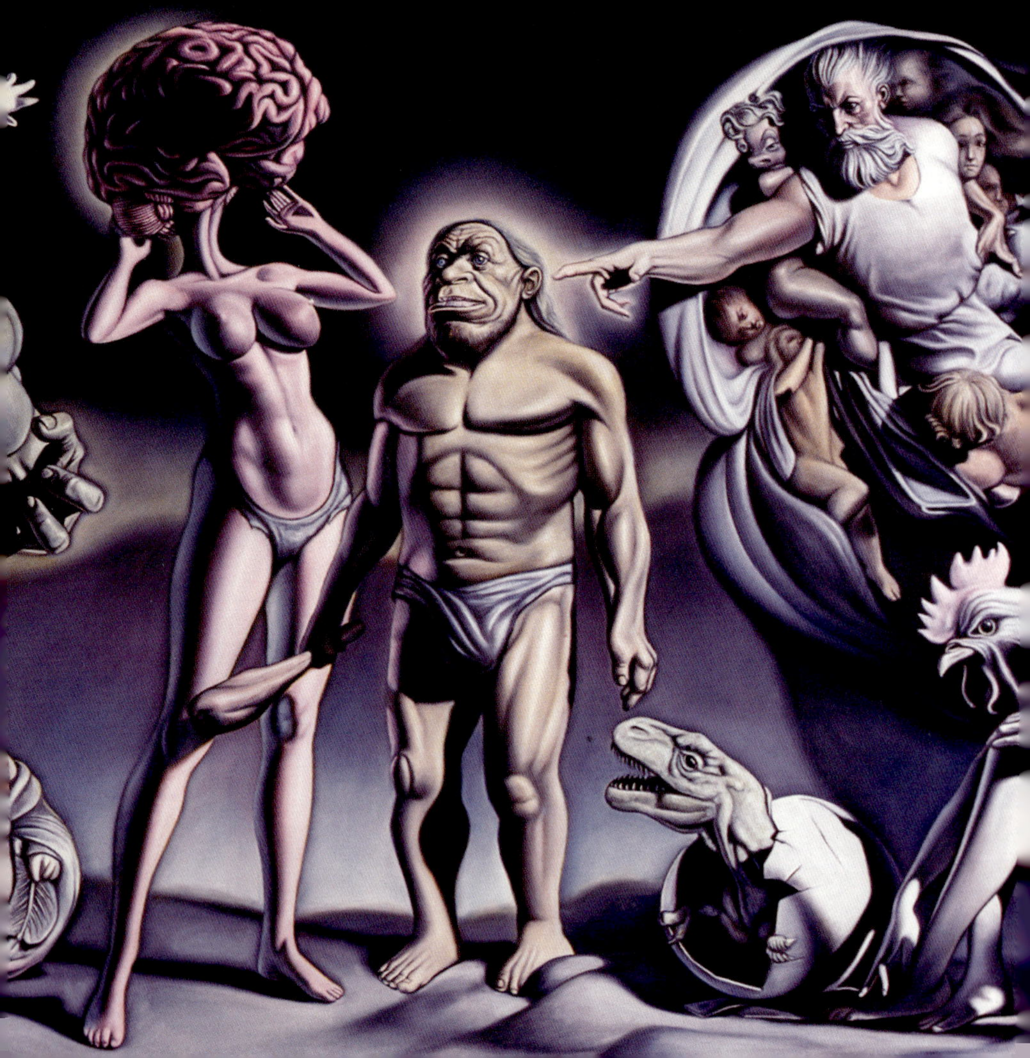

Evolution doesn't work on creationists.

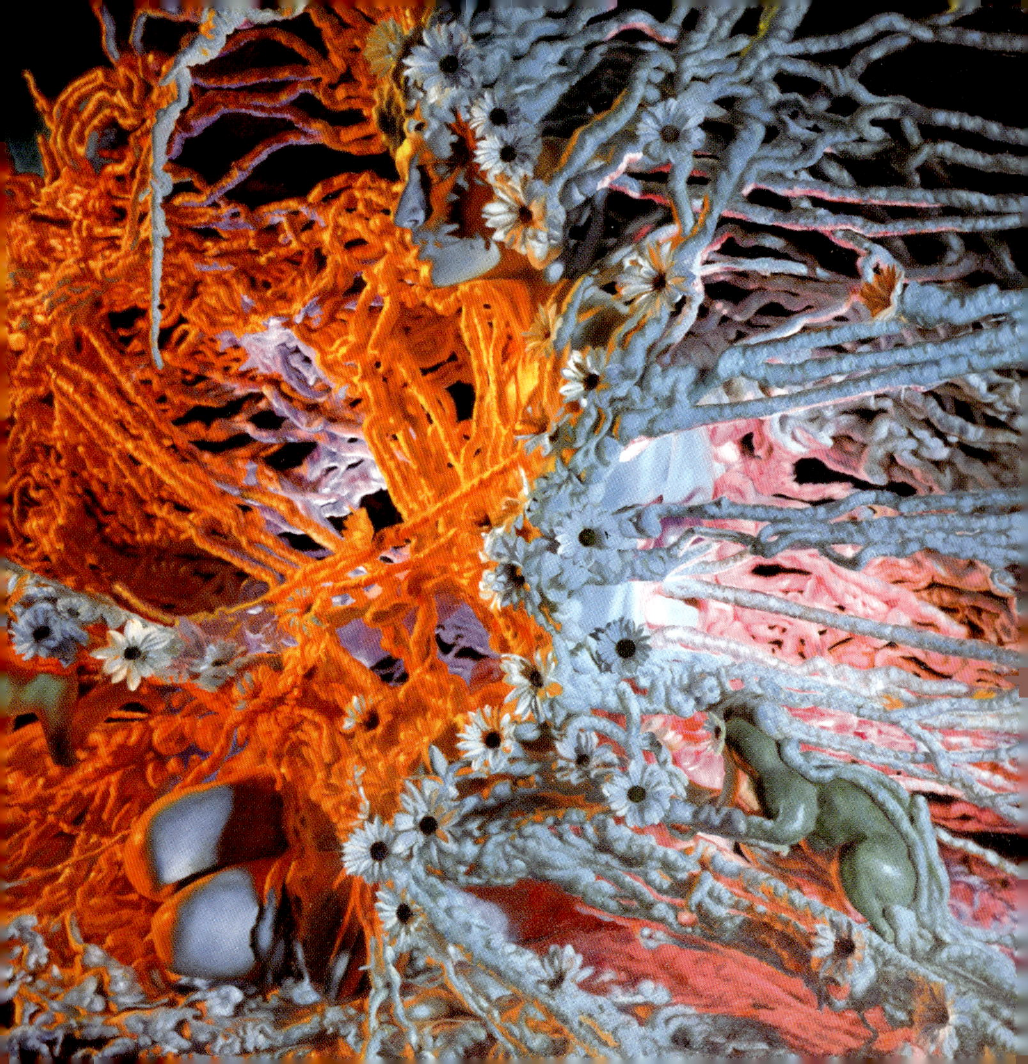

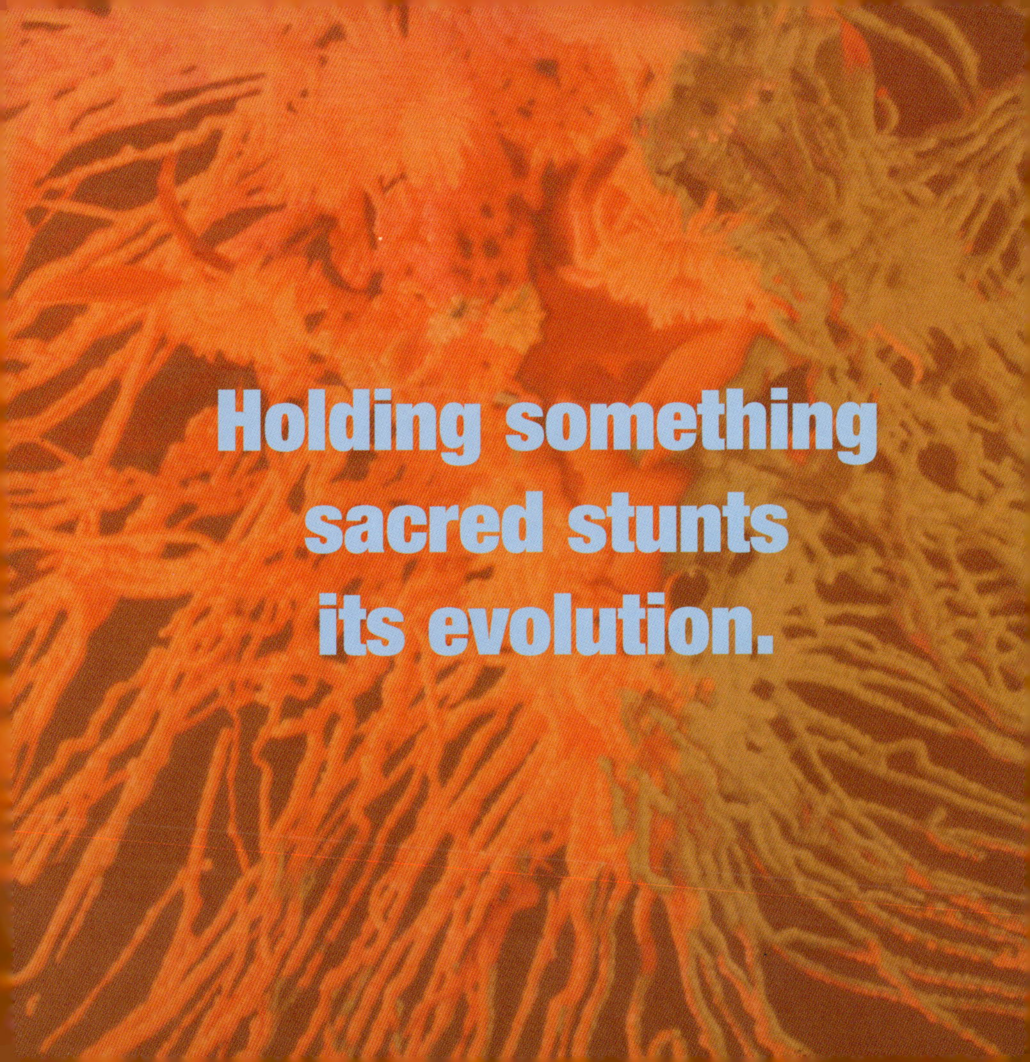
Holding something
sacred stunts
its evolution.

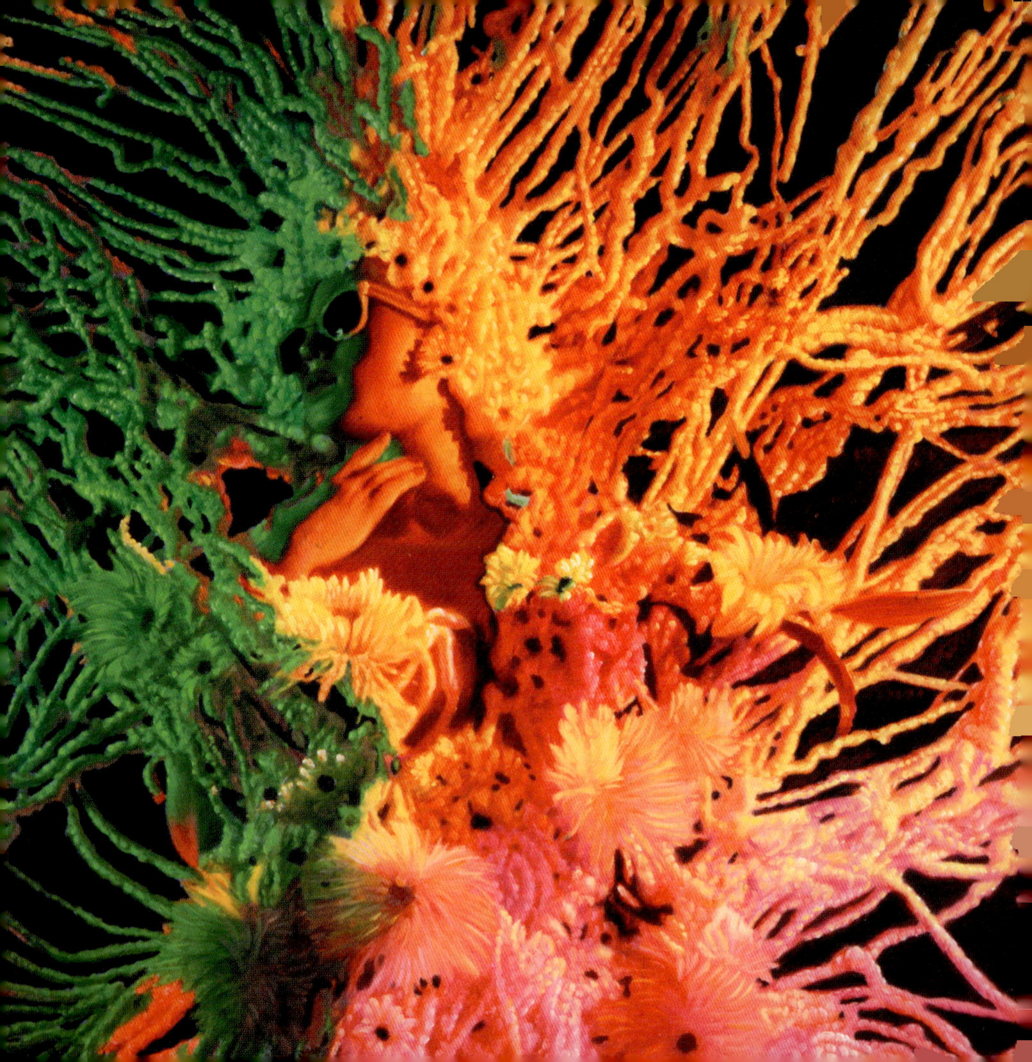

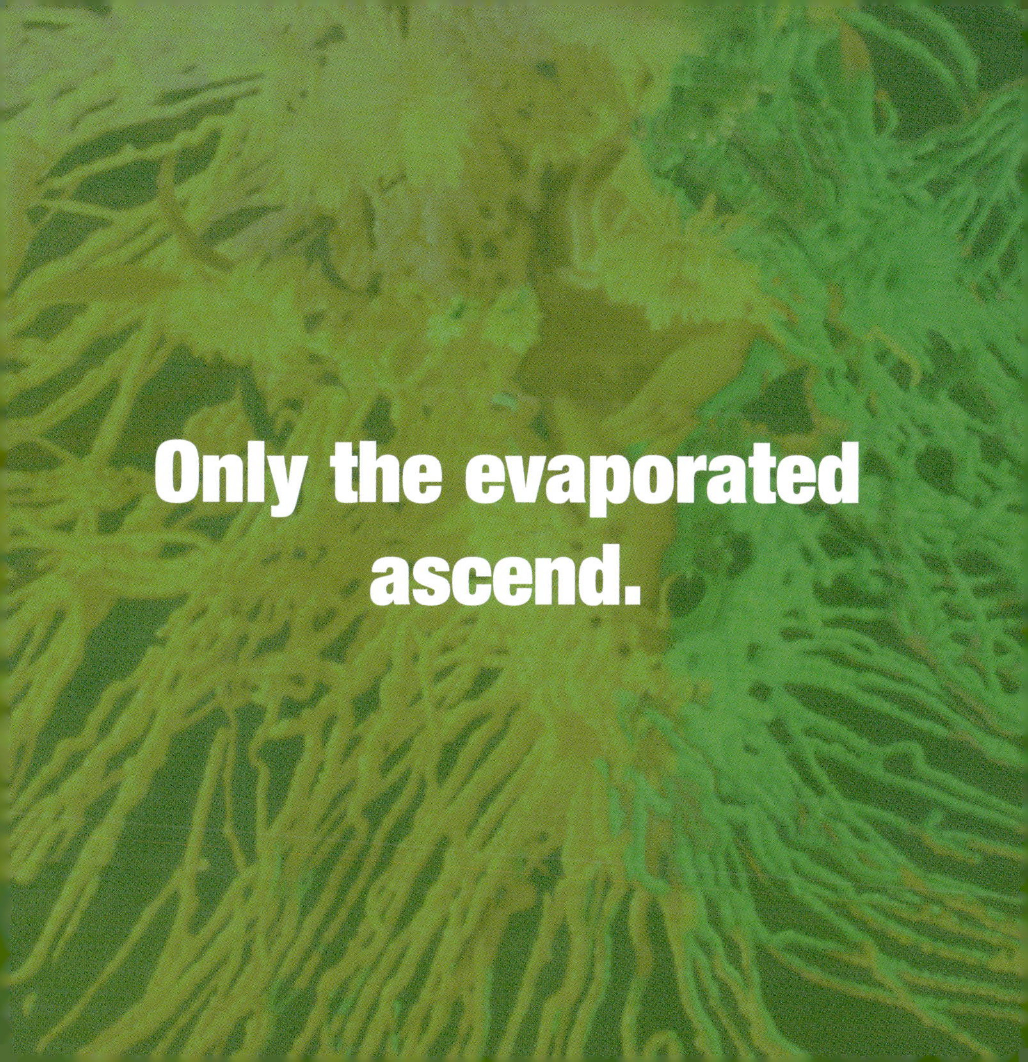
Only the evaporated
ascend.

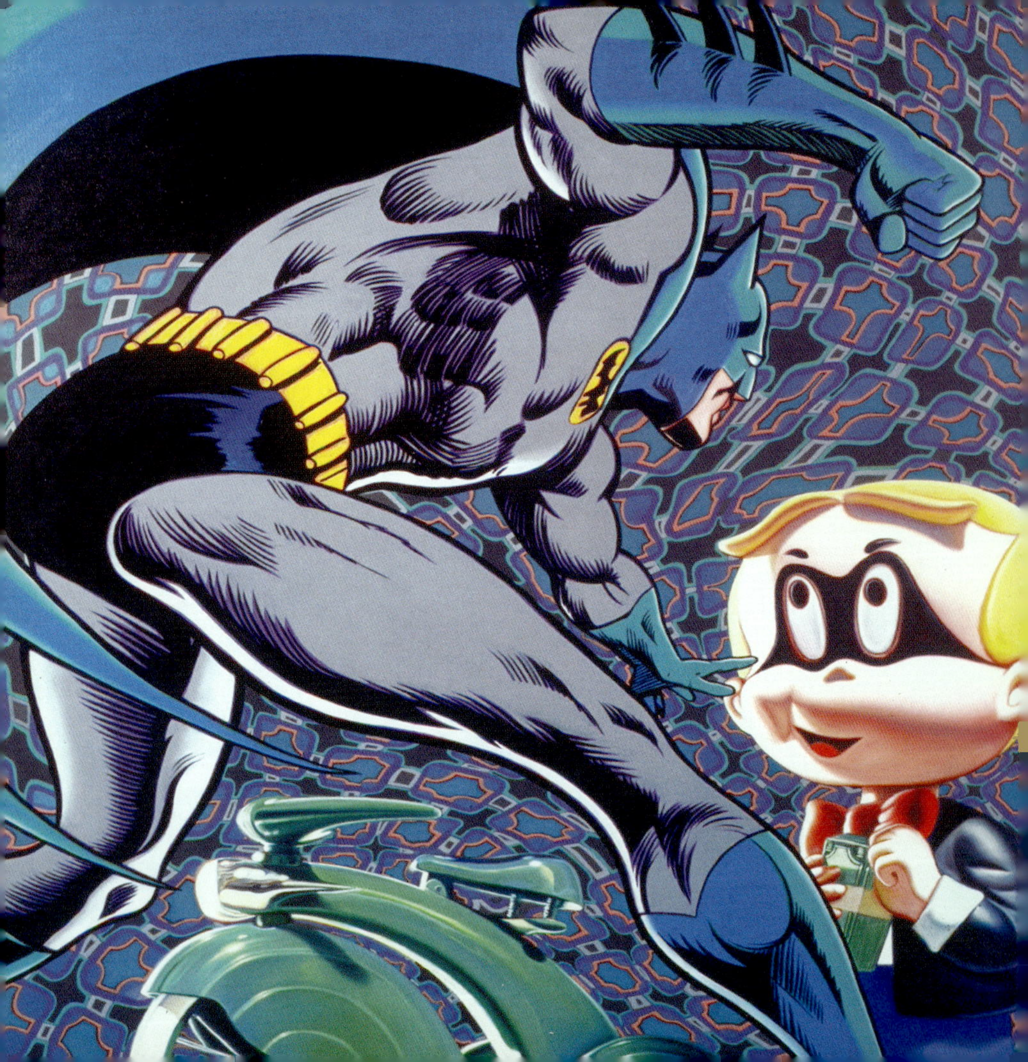

The rich don't start revolutions.

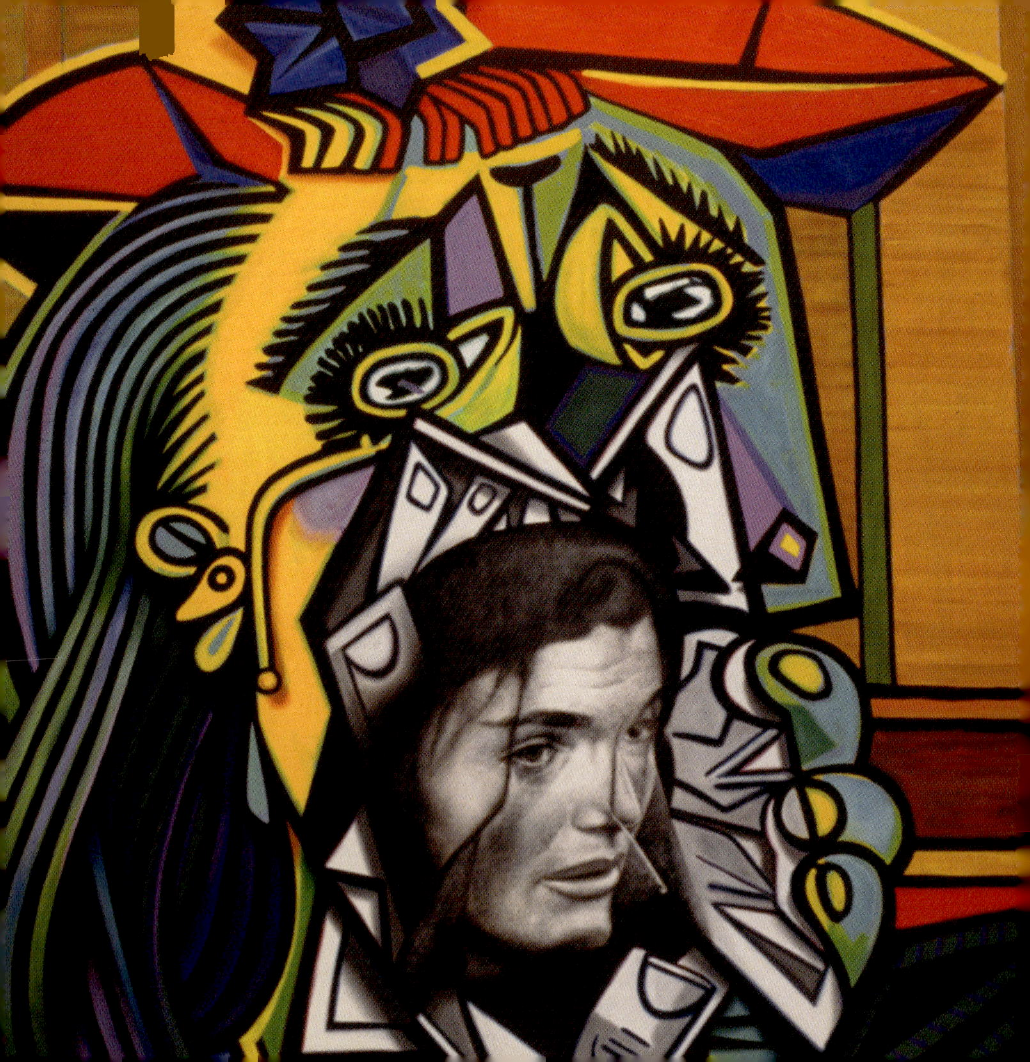

Every teardrop returns to a cloud.

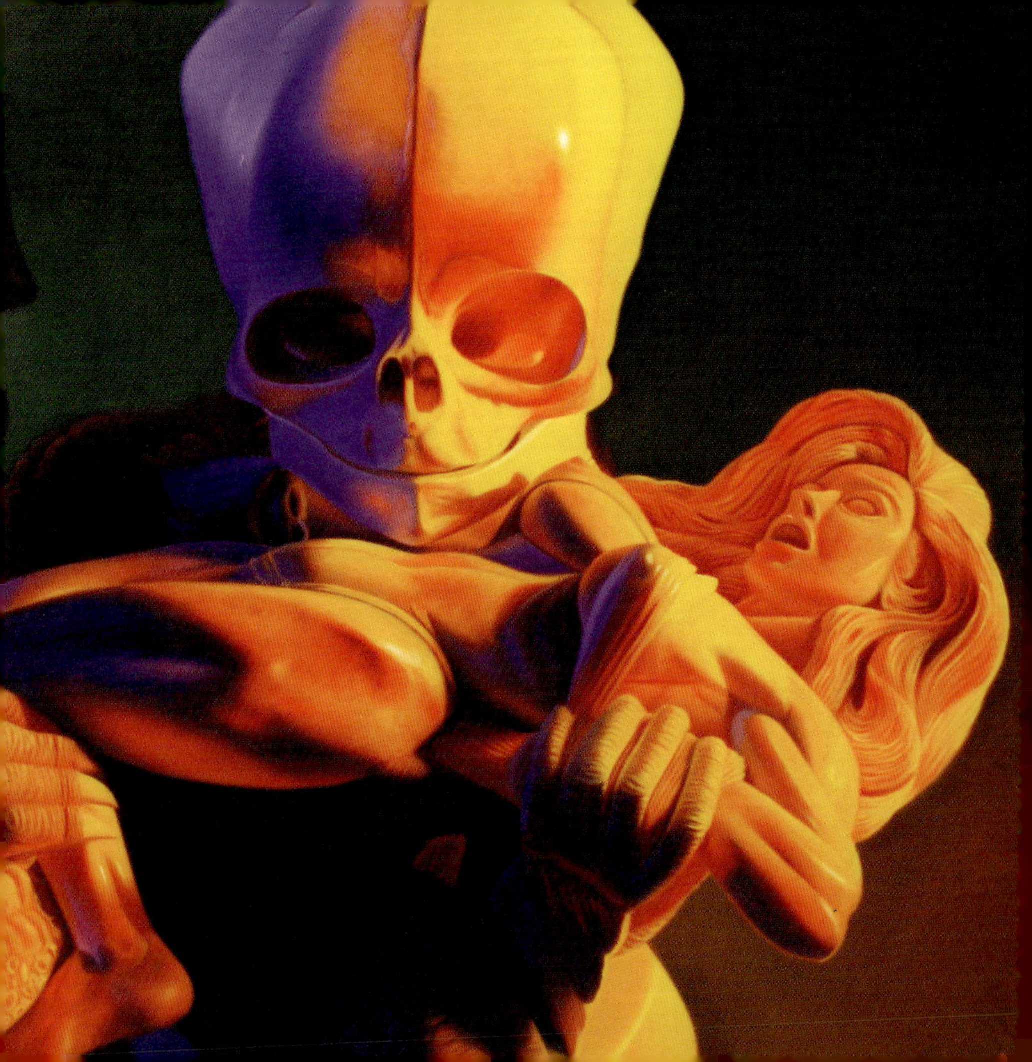

It's not God
I fear
but the woman who
bore him.

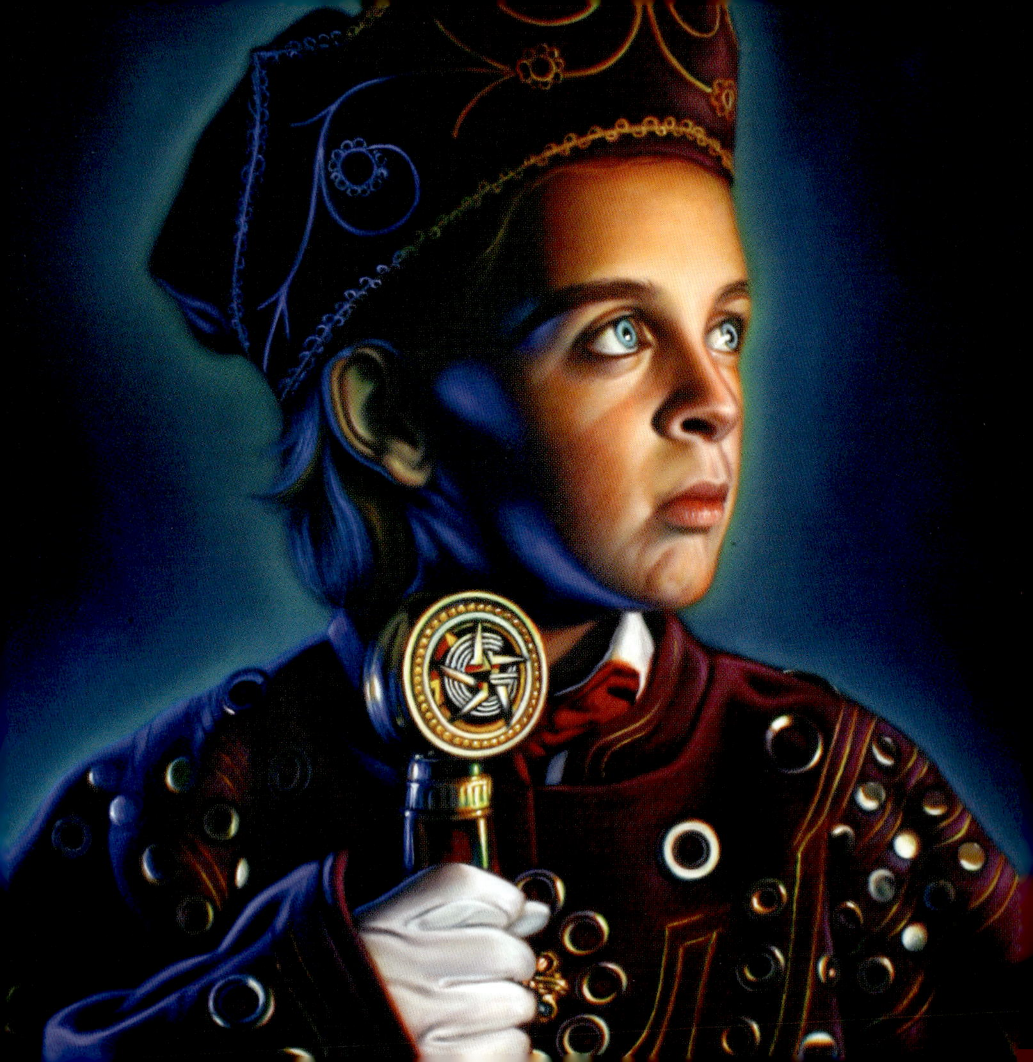

You are the dream of your ancestors.

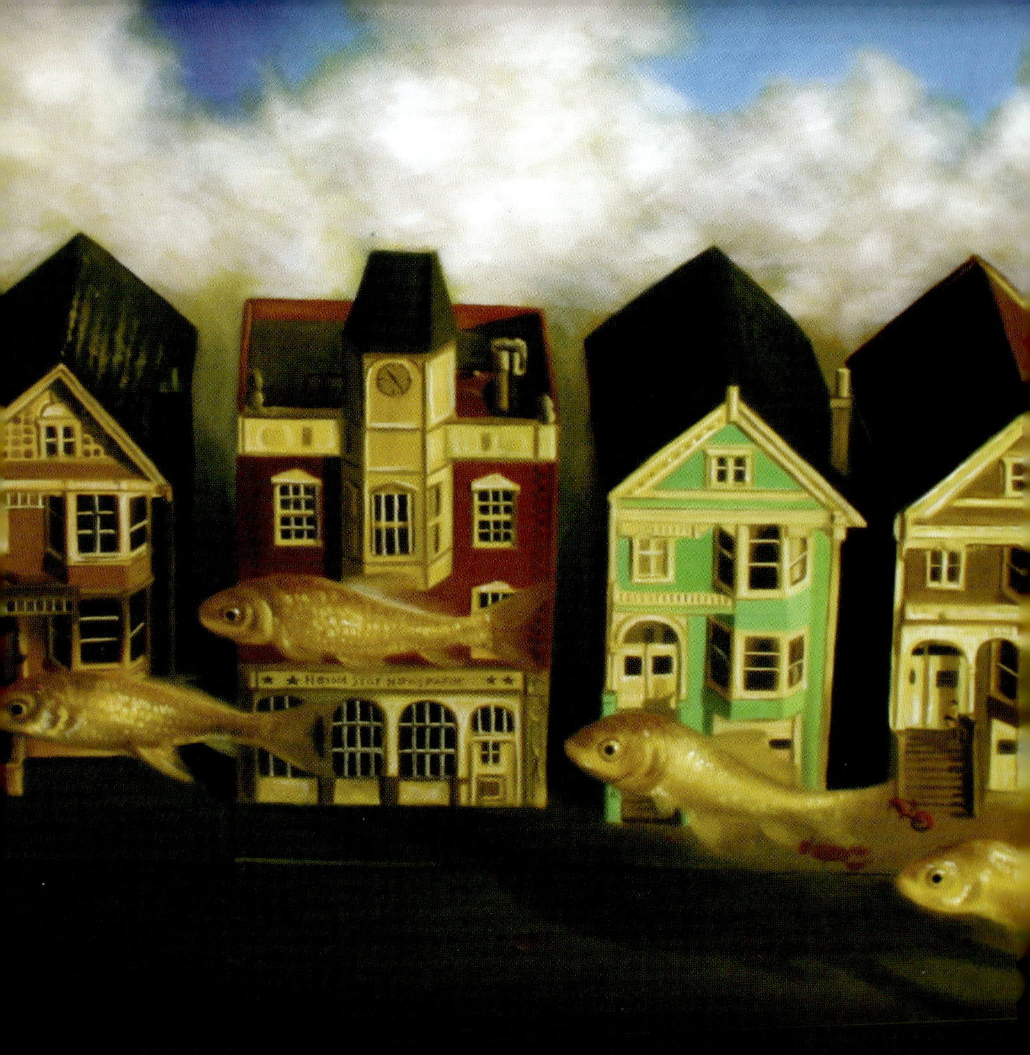

The water I breathe
would drown the
more evolved.

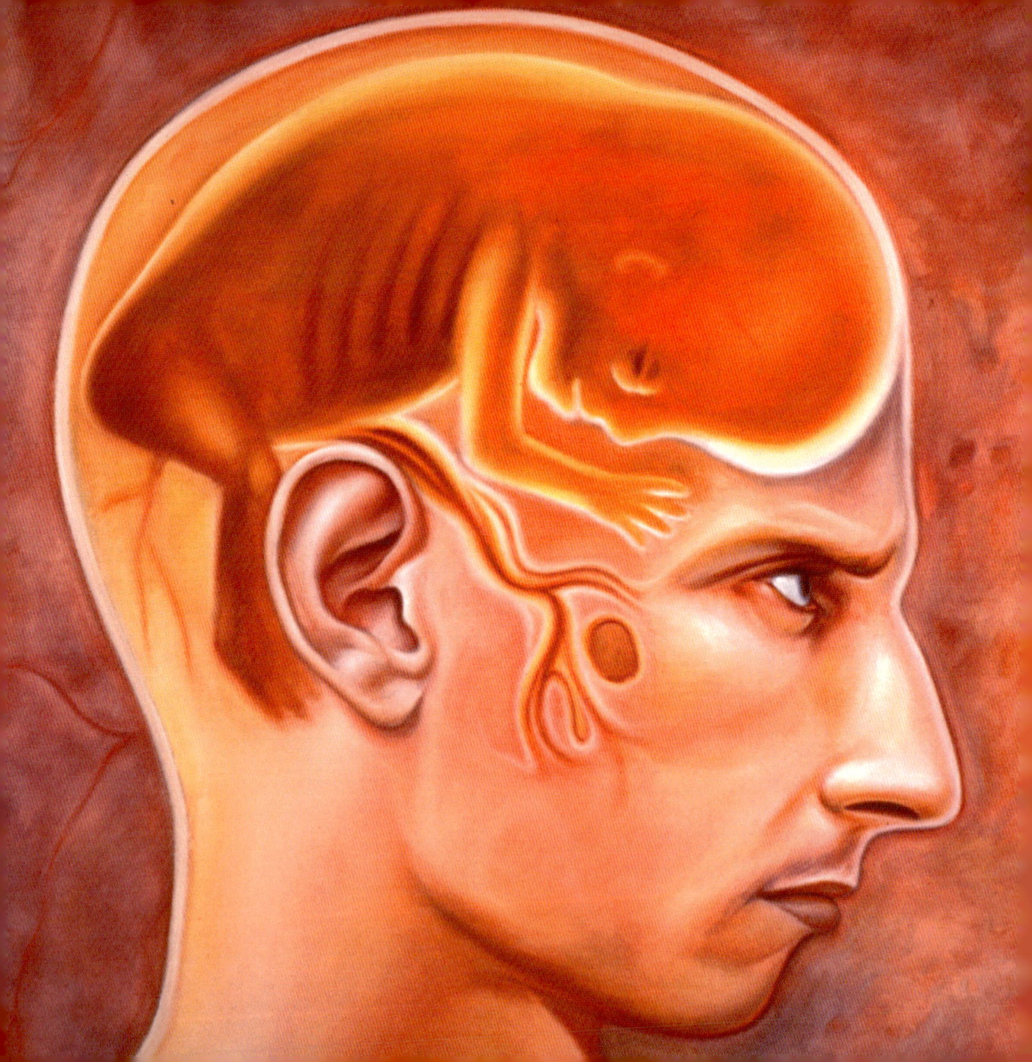

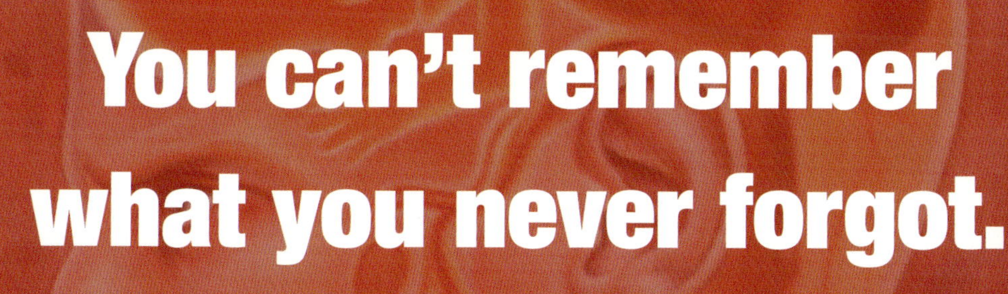
You can't remember
what you never forgot.

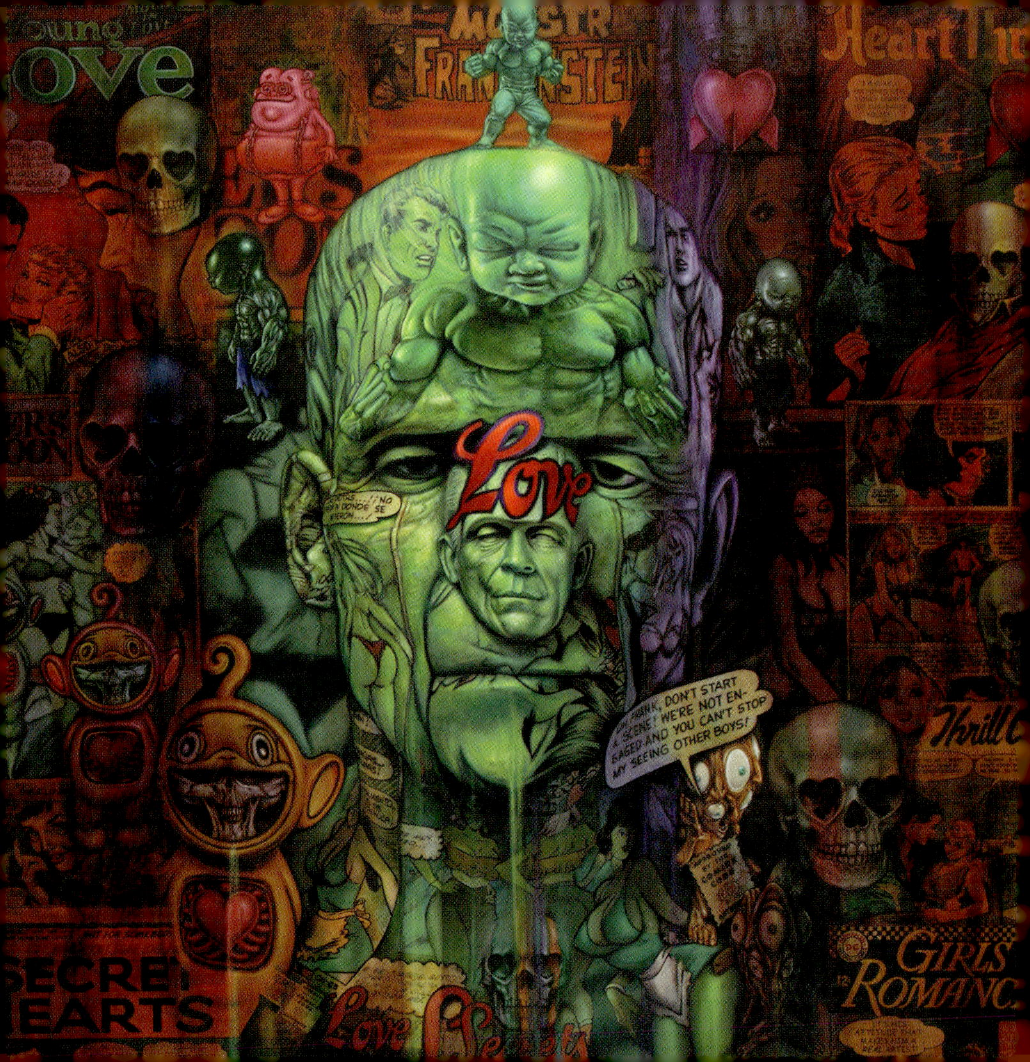

ove
MONSTR
FRANKENSTEIN
Heart
Love
OH, FRANK, DON'T START A SCENE! WE'RE NOT EN-GAGED AND YOU CAN'T STOP MY SEEING OTHER BOYS!
Thrill
GIRLS' ROMANCE
SECRET
EARTS
Love

Some people play hard to get;
I play hard to want.

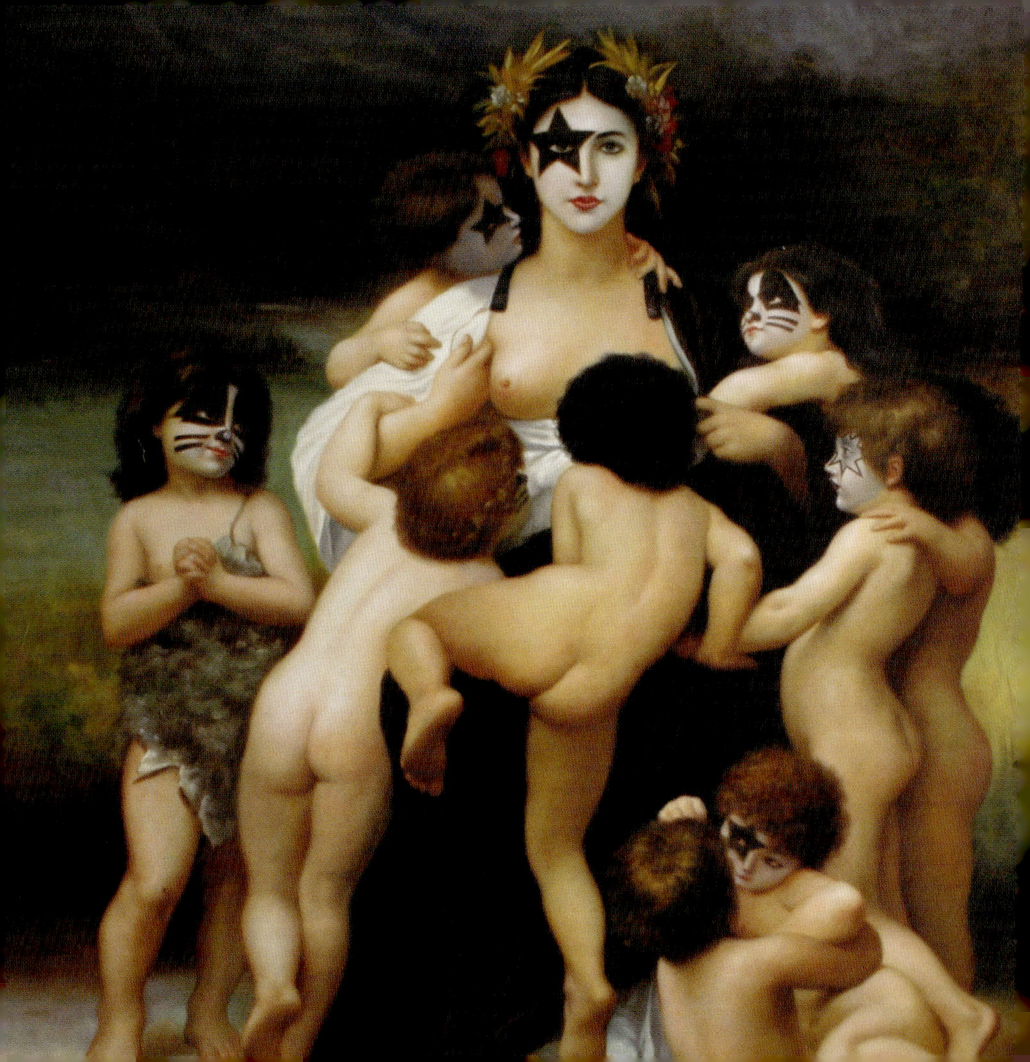

I don't love myself;
I have other people
do that for me.

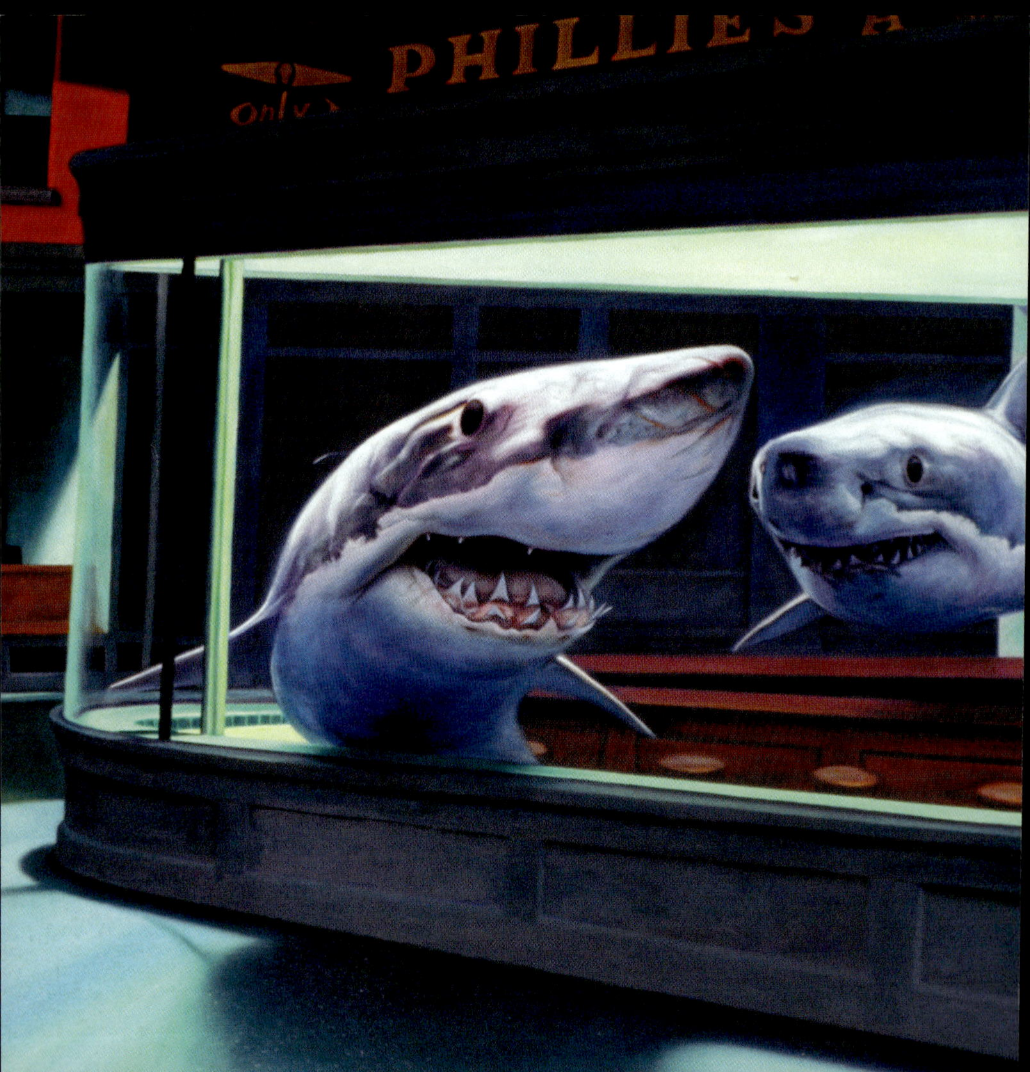
PHILLIES
Only

Jesus never walked
on water,
but he was always
on thin ice.

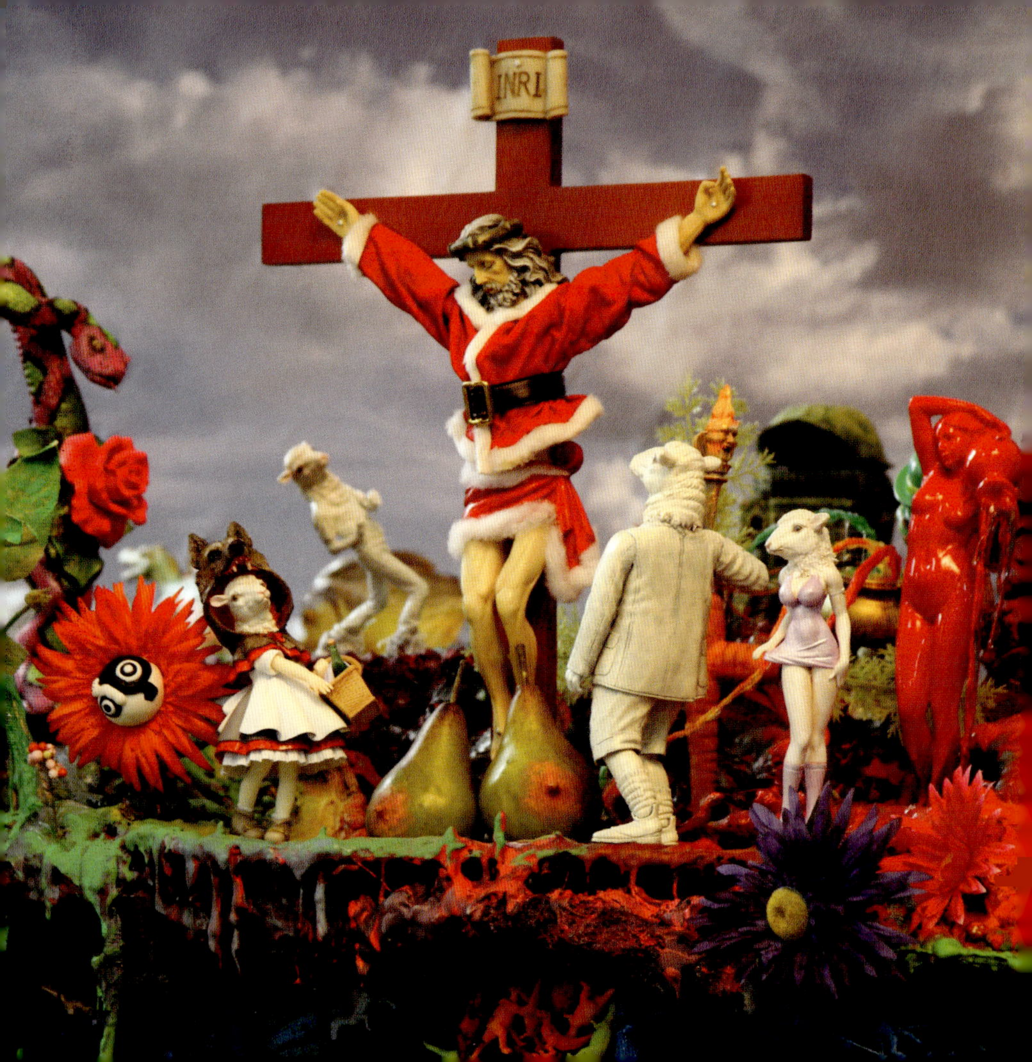
INRI

What you believe is
without a clue.

What I believe
is always true.

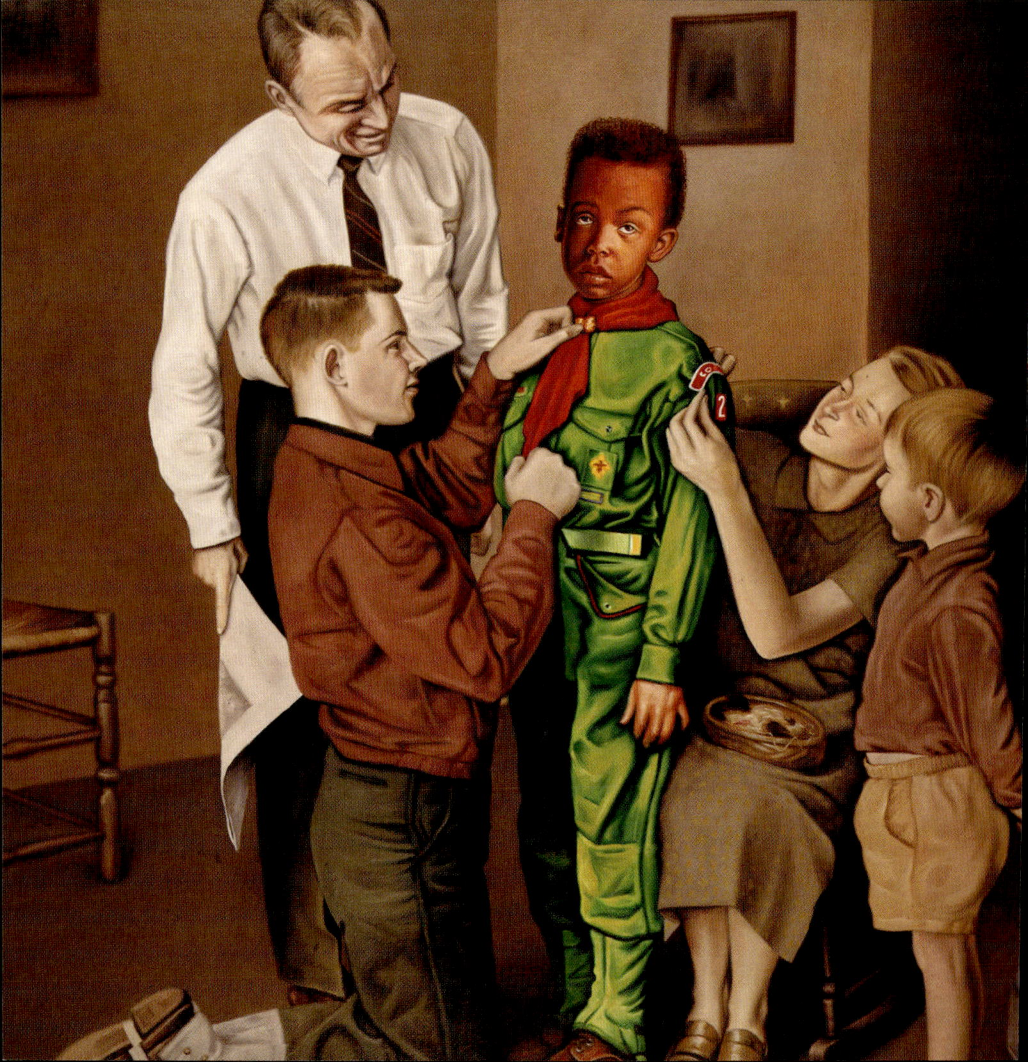
2

There is no outfit that can make me fit in.

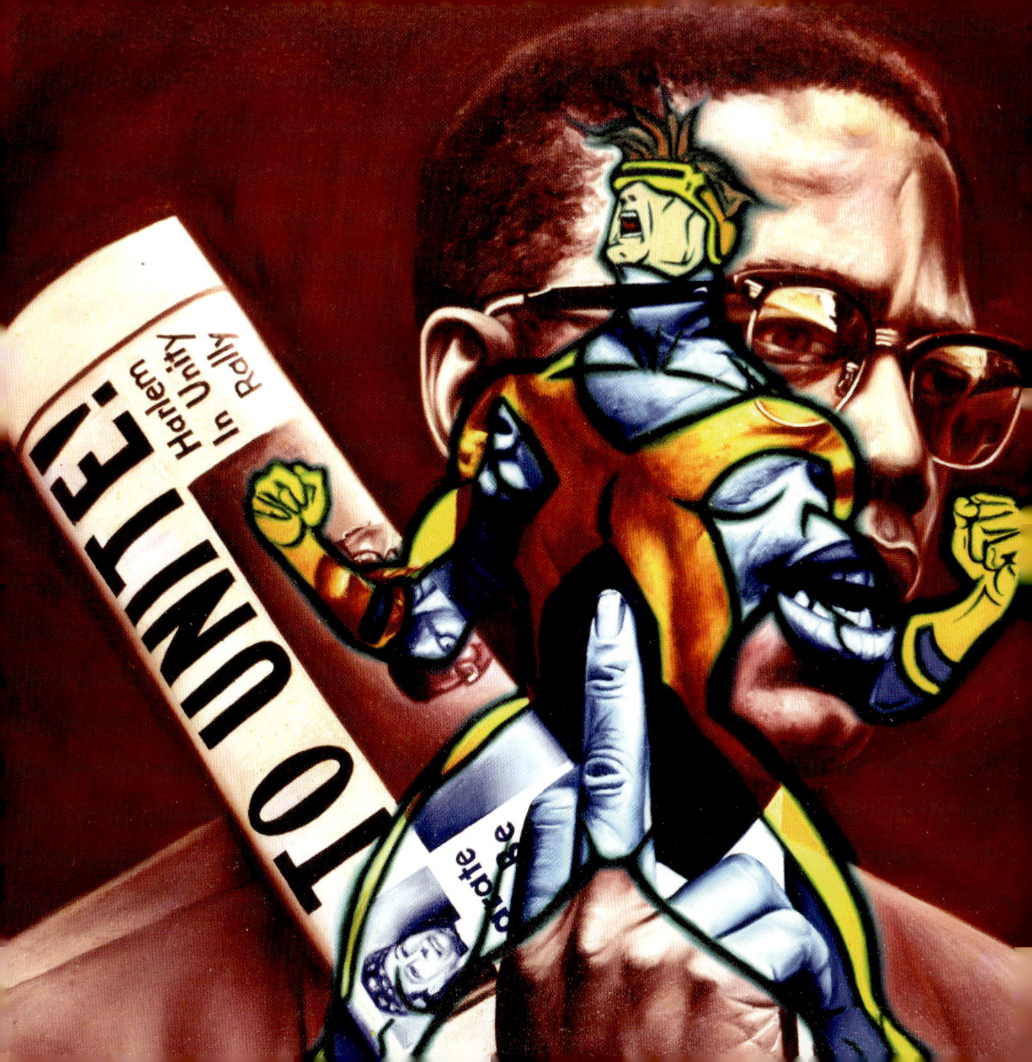
TO UNITE!
Harlem Unity In Rally

The rules always seem to be in the service of someone else.

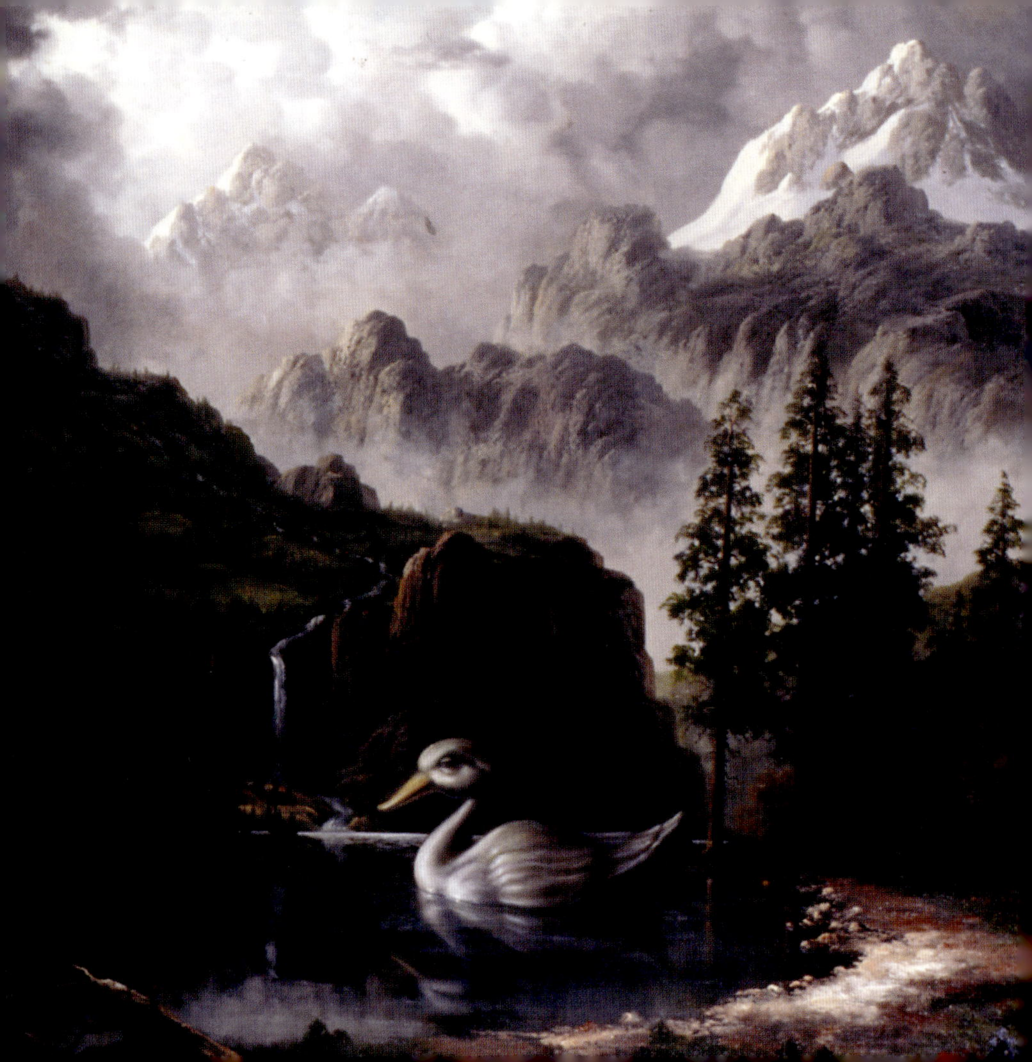

Being a big fish in a small pond is great until you have to poop.

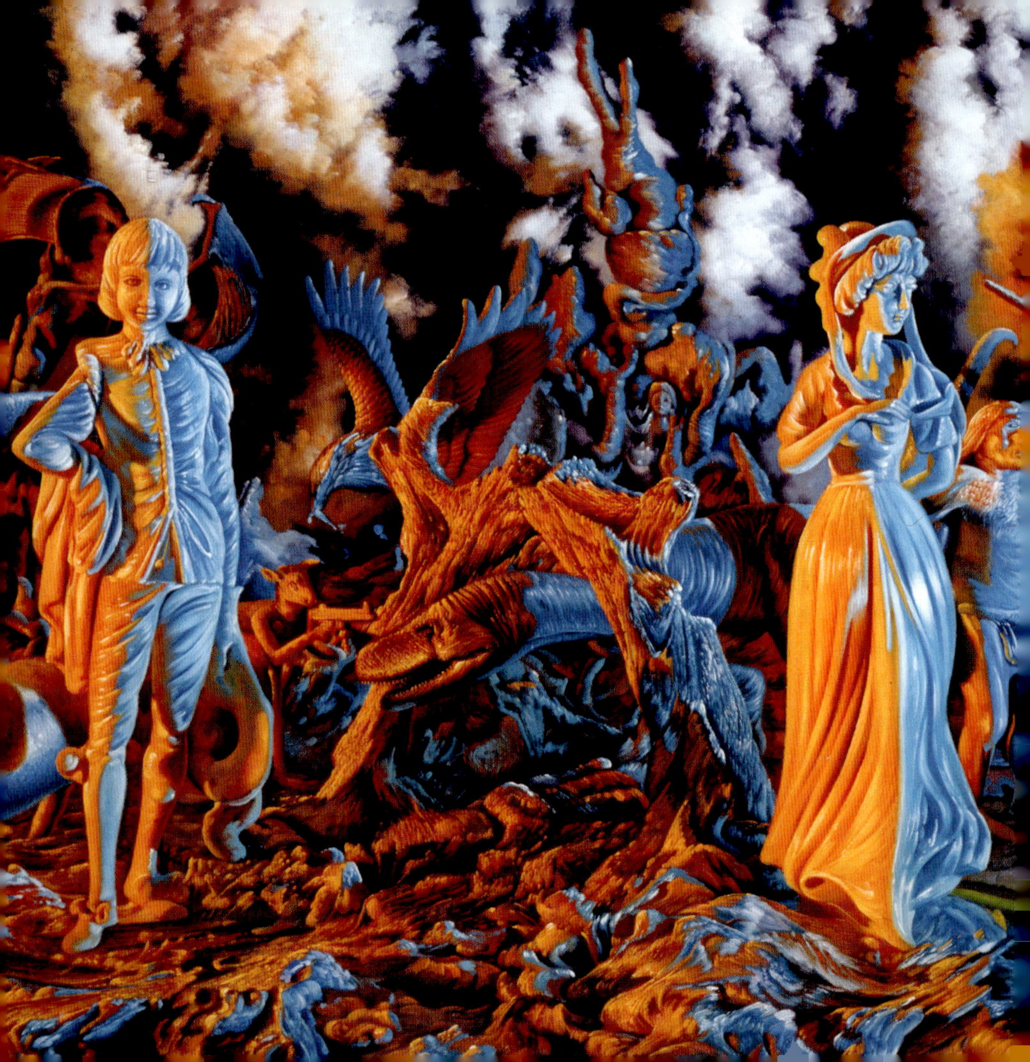

We are the offspring of extinct imagination.

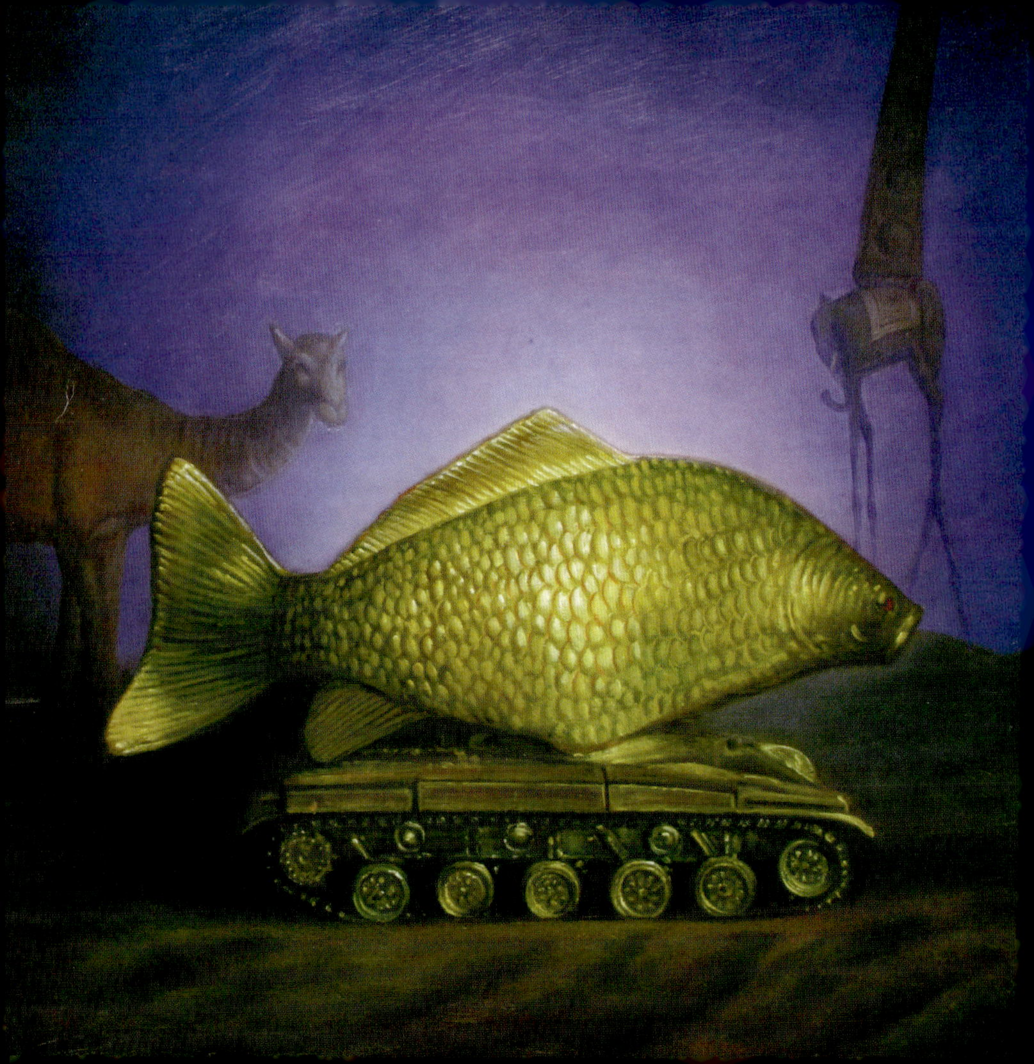

**Dreaming is easy;
I can do it in my sleep.**

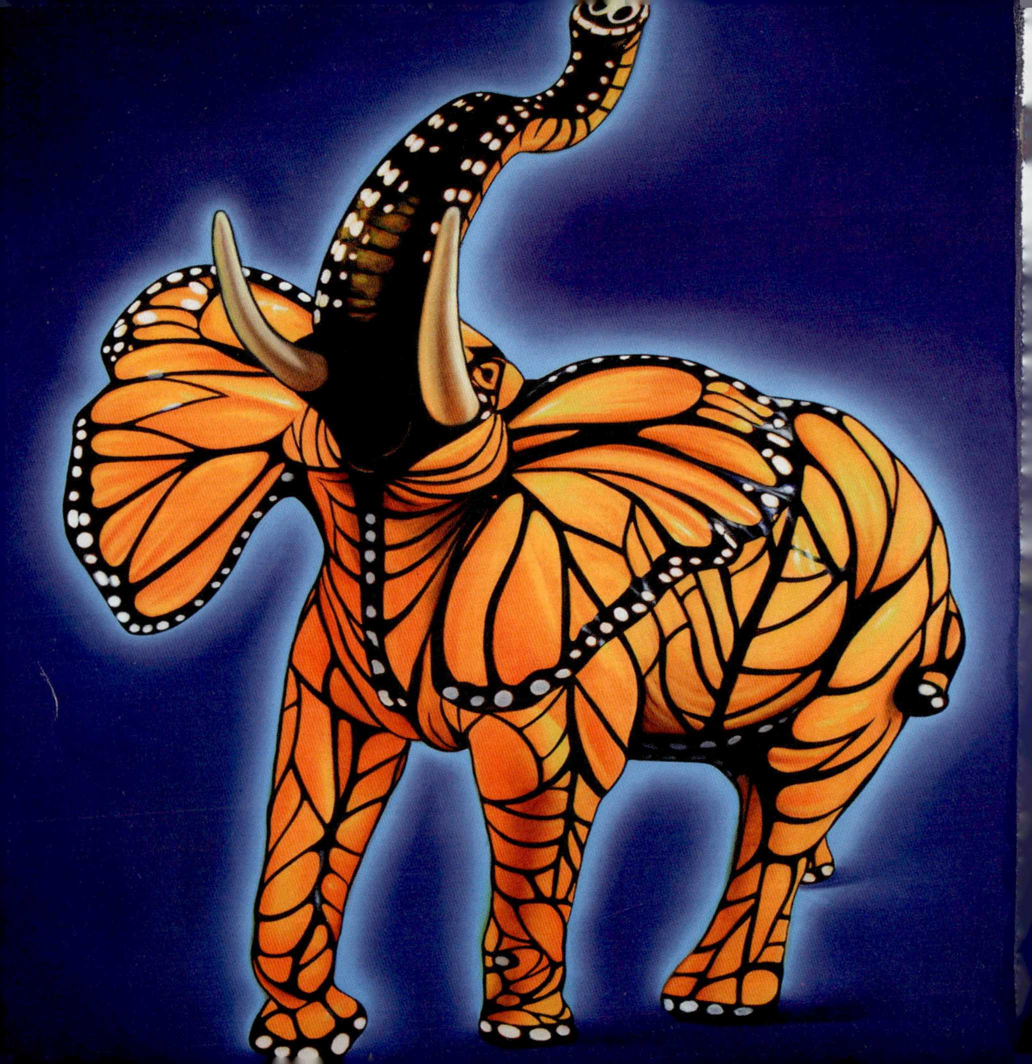